An SPC Primer

Programmed Learning Guide to Statistical Process Control Techniques

Tucson, Arizona
800-729-0867

Milwaukee, Wisconsin
414-272-8575

Current Printing (last digit)
20 19 18 17 16 15 14 13 12

9/90

ISBN 0-930011-00-7

Published by

Quality America, Inc.
Tucson, Arizona
800-729-0867
and

Milwaukee, Wisconsin
414-272-8575

INTRODUCTION

This Primer will introduce you to the most useful Statistical Process Control tools available: Control Charts. You will also be introduced to the normal probability distribution, the distribution most commonly encountered in day-to-day life. You will find very little theory in this Primer, the emphasis is on **doing.**

The format used in this primer is very simple. First you are given a "bite sized" piece of information, then you are asked to complete short exercise to test your understanding of the information. The answers to the exercises for each section are given at the end of the section. Check the answer to each exercise before moving on.

The material is divided into the three major **SECTIONS**. Each section contains a number of **FRAMES**. The index gives the SECTION and FRAME reference for major subjects.

e.g. "Decimals 1.4-1.12" means there is information about decimal numbers in section #1, frames 4 through 12 (inclusive).

TABLE OF CONTENTS

INFORMATION

1. This course will teach you several methods used to discover and control variation. We will define the process of discovering and controlling variation as "Quality Control."

2. To get all you can from this course, you should write in your best guess of the answer to the question asked in the Exercise Column. Then look up the answer. Studies have shown that people learn very quickly using this technique and they remember what they have learned very well. This method of instruction is called "Programmed Instruction." Answers are given after Frame 81.

3. The only math you need to get through this course is grade-school-level addition, subtraction, multiplication and division. A refresher course on this is included in this course.

4. When you add numbers, remember to arrange them in a column with all the decimal places in line with each other.

5. Sometimes you will need to perform some mathematical operation on a fraction. It is usually easier to work with decimal numbers. It is very easy to change a fraction to a decimal number—just divide the number on the top by the number on the bottom.

6. An example of changing a fraction to a decimal should be helpful: To change the fraction 15/64 to it's decimal equivalent, divide the top number (15) by the bottom number (64). Doing this by "long division" would get you the following results:

```
        .234375
   64 | 15.000000
        12.8
         2 20
         1 92
           280
           256
            240
            192
             480
             448
              320
              320
```

7. **Notice how zeroes are added until finally no "leftover numbers" remain; that is the remainder is zero...Now go over to the exercise column and give it a try yourself!**

EXERCISE

1. The process of discovering and controlling variation is called:

   __________ __________

2. The teaching technique used in this book is known as:

   __________ __________

3. No response required.

4. Are the numbers below ready to be added together?

   Circle One: Yes No

   12.10
   15.750
   3256.2

5. To change a fraction to a decimal, divide the __________ number by the __________ number.

6. No response required.

7. The decimal equivalent of 1/4 is: __________

   ____

INFORMATION

8. If you don't want to continue until the remainder is zero (sometimes the remainder is **never** zero!) you can "round off" the decimal to any desired number of digits. Rounding off is done by checking the digit one place to the right of the last digit you want to retain. If this digit is a five (5) or bigger, you increase the last digit you retain by one; if it is smaller than five, you leave your last retained digit unchanged.

   Decimals rounded to two digits, or any other number of digits, follow the same rules.

   Some two-digit examples:

   .5567 = .56
   .749 = .75
   .744 = .74
   .909 = .91

EXERCISE

8. Round all the decimals below to three digits.

   .3475 = ____________

   .34738 = ____________

   .2551 = ____________

   Round the decimal below to one digit:

   .745 = ____________

INFORMATION

9. When you multiply one fraction by another fraction, you have as many digits to the right of the decimal point in your answer as you had in the numbers in your problem. For example, in the problem .15 times .22, your answer will have four (4) digits to the right of the decimal points (there are two (2) digits to the right of the decimal point in each number and $2 + 2 = 4$).

EXERCISE

9. How many digits to the right of the decimal point in the following problems?

   .182 × .2 ____________

   .21 × .2 ____________

   .2112 × .3 ____________

INFORMATION

10. You will also notice that when you multiply one fraction by another (a "fraction" is any number less than one), the answer is smaller than either of the numbers multiplied. For example:

$$\begin{array}{r} .999 \\ \times .009 \\ \hline .008991 \end{array} \qquad \begin{array}{r} .001 \\ \times .01 \\ \hline .00001 \end{array} \qquad \begin{array}{r} .75 \\ \times .01 \\ \hline .0075 \end{array}$$

   Notice that the number of decimal places in the answers equals the total number of decimal places in the problem, and the answer is always less than either number multiplied.

EXERCISE

10. No response.

INFORMATION

11. You will also notice that in the problems involving .01 or .001, you could get the correct answer by moving the decimal point in the other number to the left by the same number of decimal places in the multiplier. This "trick" works for any number whose only significant digit is one (1). The examples in the response column should make this more clear.

EXERCISE

11. Multiply the following:

   21 × .1 = ____________

   21 × 10 = ____________

   21 × 100 = ____________

   21 × .01 = ____________

   21 × .001 = ____________

INFORMATION

12. The things shown in Frame 11 will be very helpful to you later on, so don't skip over it—learn it well!

   If instead of multiplying two numbers, you wish to divide one by another, and one or both of the numbers is a decimal, just arrange the numbers as you did in Frame 6 and move the decimal point in the "outside" number to the right until it is a "whole number" (no longer a fraction). Then move the decimal point on the inside number the same number of places to the right as you moved it on the outside number. Then just divide as you normally would (see Frame 6).

EXERCISE

12. Prepare the following for division by moving the decimal points:

$$22.1 \overline{)\,15\qquad}$$

$$15.55 \overline{)\,15.55\quad}$$

$$21 \overline{)\,2.1\qquad}$$

INFORMATION

13. In quality control, we use a short cut when working with some numbers by converting these numbers to "code values".

14. A code value is really just another "name" used to describe the actual number. To arrive at a code value, we just call some number zero and we describe all the other real numbers based on how they compare to zero. This can easily be demonstrated.

    Suppose an inspector was checking a part that was supposed to be a 1.000" wide ± (plus or minus) .010". He could call the reading of exactly 1.000" zero. If he was measuring with a gage marked off in .001" intervals, he would probably call the value 1.001" +1 (plus one), since it is one "gage interval" above the number he chose to call zero. Likewise, he would probably call the value .999" -1 (minus one), since it is one gage interval below zero.

15. You should note that **any** mathematical operation you can perform on actual numbers you can perform with code values. While this is an obvious time saver, there are a few new rules to keep in mind when you use code numbers.

16. It is quite common to have negative code numbers; that is, numbers below zero. While this may seem confusing, you should remember that you've been using negative numbers all your life—on the thermometer!

17. To find the distance between two numbers, if one is negative and the other is positive, you just add the two numbers together; ignoring the negative sign.

18. Notice that if a number is below zero, it always has a minus sign in front of it; if the number is above zero, it could have a plus sign in front of it, but usually there is nothing in front of it.

19. To find the distance between two negative numbers, subtract the **larger** number from the **smaller** number. Remember that negative values closest to zero represent larger real values than negative numbers further away from zero.

EXERCISE

13. In quality control, actual numbers are sometimes converted to ____________________.

14. Complete the following table:

Actual Number	Code Value
1.005	+5
1.004	
1.003	
1.002	+2
1.001	+1
1.000	0
.999	-1
.998	-2
.997	
.996	-4
.995	

15. No response.

16. The ordinary thermometer has numbers below zero. That is ____________ numbers.

17. If the temperature goes from -5° F (5 degrees below zero) to 5° F (five degrees above zero), how many degrees has the temperature risen?

    ________________________ degrees

18. The number -5 is — circle one —

    Above Zero

    Below Zero

    The number 8 is — circle one —

    Above Zero

    Below Zero

INFORMATION

For example, if we assigned code values to weights of apples, we might obtain:

Weight, ounces	Code Value
12	5
11	4
10	3
9	2
8	1
7	0
6	-1
5	-2
4	-3
3	-4

It is obvious that an apple that weights in at -4 code value is smaller than an apple tipping the scale at -1. In fact, we can find out just how much smaller our first apple is by subtracting the larger value (-1) from the smaller value (-4) to get the code value answer of 3—which converts directly to a real value of 3-ounce difference between our apples.

20. You no doubt remember that the distance between two positive numbers is found simply by subtracting the smaller number from the larger number; but do the exercises in the exercise column just to refresh your memory.

21. In quality control, the distance between two numbers is called the "RANGE", often abbreviated to just the letter R.

22. The two numbers we are usually interested in in quality control are the highest and lowest values found in a sample. Keeping in mind the rules we just reviewed concerning positive and negative numbers, compute the sample ranges in the exercise column.

If you don't get all of the responses correct and understand why, you'd better back up: **This is very important!!**

23. Whenever you work with code values, you will want to know how you can convert your answers back to actual values. With ranges this is done by finding the "class interval" (simply the real value that corresponds to zero subtracted from the real value that corresponds to +1), and multiplying the code value answer by this class interval.

EXERCISE

19. Compute the distance between the following negative numbers:

-6 to -11 =

-3 to - 1 =

-7 to -15 =

-2 to 0 =

-2 to - 3 =

-5 to - 9 =

-9 to - 5 =

-5 to - 2 =

20. Compute the distances between the numbers below:

5 to 15 =
16 to 7 =
0 to 8 =

21. What does the letter "R" stand for?

____

22. Compute R for the following sets of sample values:

Set One: -4, 5, 5, -1, -1

R = ______________________

Set Two: -7, 5, 8, 3, 0

R = ______________________

Set Three: -1, 0, -5, -9, 0

R = ______________________

INFORMATION

Let's do this with the data from Frame 14. We have the following assignments:

Diameter, inches	Code value
1.005	5
1.004	4
1.003	3
1.002	2
1.001	1
1.000	0
.999	–1
.998	–2
.997	–3
.996	–4
.995	–5

A sample of five (5) parts gives the coded measurements: -3, 0, 0, 2, 3.

The sample R = 6 in code values, but the shop foreman wants the "real" range. No problem! First, subtract the actual value of zero (1.000") from the actual value of +1 (1.001") to get the class interval of .001". Then, multiply your code value answer (6) by the class interval to find the actual value of the range: $.001 \times 6 = .006$. Try it!

EXERCISE

23. Convert the code ranges to real ranges, assume the table in the information column represents your values.

Code	Real
7	_____
5	_____
3	_____

24. In quality control, an individual measurement is usually identified by the letter x.

24. What letter is commonly used to identify an individual measurement?

____

25. You now know two quality control symbols: X, which identifies an individual measurement; and the symbol used to represent sample range, R.

25. What symbol represents the distance from the high sample value to the low sample value?

____

26. "Averages" are very common in quality control. An average (sometimes called the "mean") of a set of numbers is very easy to compute; all you do is add the numbers together and divide the total by the number of individual values. Assume you wanted to compute the average of the following values:

1, 7, 9, 8, –1, –6, –3, 0, –5, 1

Step one is to add all the numbers, a trick is to first add all the negative numbers separately:

–1, –6, –3, –5 = –15 total

Then, all the positive numbers:

1 + 7 + 9 + 8 + 1 = 26 total.

The grand total is then:

26 – 15 = 11 total

And the number of pieces measured is then (10) — determined by just counting.

The average is computed by dividing the sum of the measurements by the number of measurements, or:

$$\begin{array}{r} 1.1 \\ 10\overline{)11.0} \\ \underline{10} \\ 1.0 \end{array}$$

Try it yourself in the exercise column.

26. Find the averages.

Set One

1, 3, 5, –7, –8

Average =

_____ ⌐____ = _____

Set Two

1, 1, 1, 1, 1

Average =

_____ ⌐____ = _____

Set Three

–2, –3, –6, –5, –4

Average =

_____ ⌐____ = _____

Set Four

3, 6, 2, 5, 4

Average =

_____ ⌐____ = _____

INFORMATION

27. Did you notice that whenever the total is a negative number the average is negative, too?

    This is very important to remember. Also remember that if you multiply two numbers and only one of them is negative, the product (answer) is negative.

28. In quality control, when we wish to identify an average, we usually just put a line above the symbol of the numbers we are averaging. In the previous frames, we were averaging individual measurements, symbolically identified as X; thus, the average is symbolically identified as $\overline{X}$ (called X bar).

29. Using the logic in Frame 28, do the exercise in the exercise column.

30. In quality control (QC from here on out), it is even common to compute the average of a group of $\overline{X}$'s. True to form, we identify this as $\overline{\overline{X}}$, but to avoid sounding too silly, we refer to this as the Grand Average, or X double bar, not X bar bar.

31. With averages, as with ranges, we usually work with code values; thus, there is always the chance that we will need to convert our answer back to its real value. Refer to Frame 23 and review the procedure we use to convert a code value for R to a real value.

    To convert a code value for $\overline{X}$ to its real value, we use a similar procedure. However, we may now have a **negative** code value (the value of R is never negative) and you must remember that a positive number (your class interval is always positive) times a negative number always yields a negative answer. The reason it is so important to remember the negative sign will become clear shortly.

32. A "shorthand" commonly used by everyone involved in math is the "formula". A formula is simply a symbolic way of saying something: For example, instead of saying "one plus two equals three", we can write 1 + 2 = 3.

33. It is easier to write formulas than sentences, in the formula. For example, our method of computing averages could be written as:

$$\overline{X} = \sum_{i=1}^{n} \frac{X_i}{n}$$

Where:

$\overline{X}$ = average of several X's

X_i = an individual x measurement

n = the number of individual X's

ending value / starting value $\sum_{i=1}^{n}$ = a symbol meaning "sum of" all the individual values starting with the first value (i = 1) and ending with the last value (n).

In words, this formula says "The average of several X's ($\overline{X}$) equals (=) the sum total (Σ) of the individual X's (X_i) divided by (—) the number of individual X's (n).

EXERCISE

27. The answer to

    -5 times 6 is

    circle one:

    negative   positive

28. Write the correct pronunciation of the symbol $\overline{X}$.

    ____

29. Write the symbol and pronunciation for an average of a group of ranges:

    ____

30. The usual pronunciation of the symbol $\overline{\overline{X}}$ is X bar bar, true or false?

    ____

31. Is it possible to get a value R = -6?

    circle one:

    yes   no

32. If we write 2 + 5 = X we have written a:

    ____

33. Write the symbol meaning "sum of" all the values:

    ____

INFORMATION

34. Let's start right off using symbols to tell us how to convert a code value of $\overline{X}$ to a real value. Quite simply, the formula is:

$$\overline{X}_A = O_A + (\overline{X}_C)\ (i)$$

Where: $\overline{X}_A$ = actual average

O_A = actual number assigned to code value zero

$\overline{X}_C$ = sample average in code values

i = class interval

The correct way to say this in words is "the average in actual numbers ($\overline{X}_A$) equals (=) the actual value of code value zero (O_A) plus the code value of the average ($\overline{X}_C$) times the class interval (i)".

35. Do you see why we said in Frame 27 that it was important to keep track of the negative sign when computing averages? Obviously, adding a negative number is the equivalent of subtracting a positive number. Check the exercise column.

36. The principle above sounds complicated, but it is very important. Perhaps the best way to grasp the concept is to work with it a bit; review the examples below, then go to the exercise column and see how well you've got it.

Set A		Set B		Set C	
−5	9	14	−18	−3	0
+9	−5	−18	+14	+0	−3
4	4	− 4	− 4	−3	−3

Notice that no matter how you arrange the numbers, you get the same answer; use this "trick" if one arrangement makes sense to you and the other doesn't.

37. How about a review of what you've learned so far? You now know how to work with code values, both positive and negative. Using the basic mathematical operations (adding, subtracting, multiplying, and dividing), you can compute the range, average, average range, and grand average of any set of sample measurements. You also know the meanings of the following symbols:

X = an individual measurement

$\overline{X}$ = (X bar) The average of a series of individual values.

$\overline{\overline{X}}$ = (X double bar) the "grand average", an average of a series of averages

R = the range (highest sample values minus lowest sample values) of a sample

$\overline{R}$ = (R bar) the average of a series of ranges

EXERCISE

34. Compute the real value of the average ($\overline{X}_A$) given the following information:

O_A = 1.000"

$\overline{X}_C$ = −2.0

i = .001"

$\overline{X}_A$ = ________

35. Work the following problems:

+3 − 1 = ________

3 + (−1) = ________

6 − 7 = ________

6 + (−7) = ________

36. Work the following problems:

−9 − 9 = ________

−9 + 9 = ________

−9 + 10 = ________

10 − 9 = ________

9 − 9 = ________

−9 + 10 = ________

9 − 10 = ________

−10 + 9 = ________

37. No response.

i = class interval

$\overline{X}_A$ = actual average

O_A = actual number assigned to code value "0"

$\overline{X}_C$ = sample average in code values

INFORMATION

38. You might notice that the things you've learned simply help you to organize data. In fact, that is about half the battle. Organized data is much easier to interpret and analyze. Our next step is another organization step—plotting your sample data on a graph. This graph is the beginning of the "Control Chart" you've heard so much about.

39. Below, you will see the rudimentary beginnings of a control chart: Study it carefully.

AVERAGES AND RANGES CHART

Specification and Tolerance: 1.000 ± .010
Zero Equals: 1.000
Class Interval: .001"

PART NAME

PART NUMBER | START DATE

SAMPLE MEASUREMENTS		1	2	3	4	5	6
	1	5	0	-8	-4	0	-6
	2	8	-6	2	-8	3	-3
	3	7	5	-3	-9	0	1
	4	-4	-3	1	4	5	8
	5	-2	0	2	-3	4	5
SUM		14	-4	-6	-20	12	5
AVERAGE, $\bar{X}$		2.8	-0.8	-1.2	-4	2.4	1
RANGE, R		12	11	10	13	5	14

Notice that this employs only the basic principles learned already.

40. Complete the chart for the sample data.

EXERCISE

38. Basically, a control chart is a ____________ of organized sample data.

39. No response.

40. Show chart for samples 1 through 25.

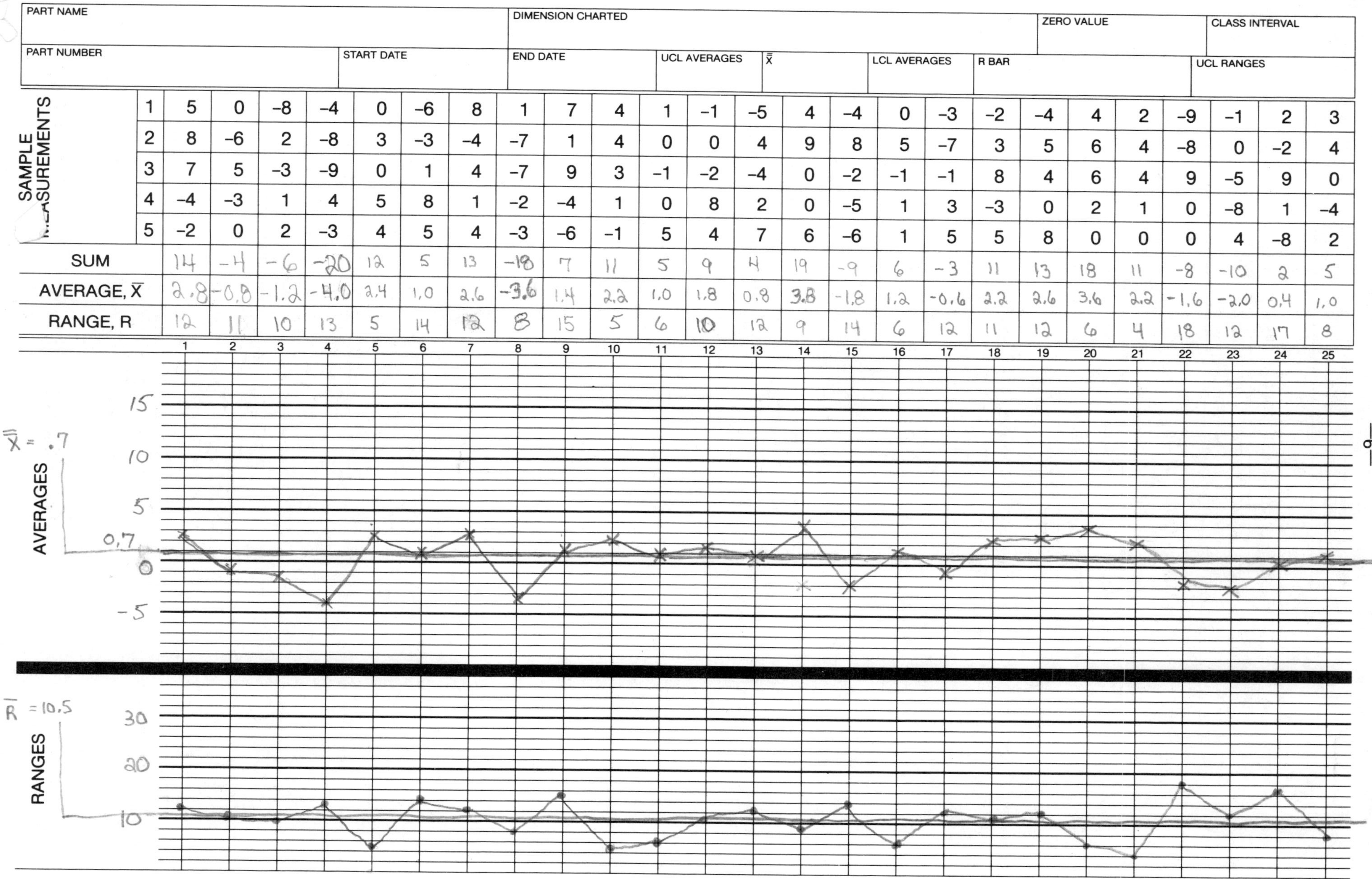

QUALITY AMERICA, INC.®

CONTROL CHARTS FOR AVERAGES AND RANGES

PART NAME	DIMENSION CHARTED	ZERO VALUE	CLASS INTERVAL

PART NUMBER	START DATE	END DATE	UCL AVERAGES	$\bar{\bar{X}}$	LCL AVERAGES	R BAR	UCL RANGES

SAMPLE MEASUREMENTS	1	2	3	4	5	6	7	8	9	10	11	12	13	14	15	16	17	18	19	20	21	22	23	24	25
1	5	0	−8	−4	0	−6	8	1	7	4	1	−1	−5	4	−4	0	−3	−2	−4	4	2	−9	−1	2	3
2	8	−6	2	−8	3	−3	−4	−7	1	4	0	0	4	9	8	5	−7	3	5	6	4	−8	0	−2	4
3	7	5	−3	−9	0	1	4	−7	9	3	−1	−2	−4	0	−2	−1	−1	8	4	6	4	9	−5	9	0
4	−4	−3	1	4	5	8	1	−2	−4	1	0	8	2	0	−5	1	3	−3	0	2	1	0	−8	1	−4
5	−2	0	2	−3	4	5	4	−3	−6	−1	5	4	7	6	−6	1	5	5	8	0	0	0	4	−8	2
SUM	14	−4	−6	−20	12	5	13	−18	7	11	5	9	4	19	−9	6	−3	11	13	18	11	−8	−10	2	5
AVERAGE, $\bar{X}$	2.8	−0.8	−1.2	−4.0	2.4	1.0	2.6	−3.6	1.4	2.2	1.0	1.8	0.8	3.8	−1.8	1.2	−0.6	2.2	2.6	3.6	2.2	−1.6	−2.0	0.4	1.0
RANGE, R	12	11	10	13	5	14	12	8	15	5	6	10	12	9	14	6	12	11	12	6	4	18	12	17	8

CALCULATION WORK SHEET

RANGES CHART

Subgroups Included: ______________________

Sum of Ranges = S =

Number of Subgroups = K =

Subgroup Size = n =

Average Range = $\bar{R} = \frac{S}{K}$ = __________ = [ ]

D_3 factor =

$LCL_R = D_3\bar{R}$ = (   )(   ) = [ ]

D_4 factor =

$UCL_R = D_4\bar{R}$ = (   )(   ) = [ ]

AVERAGES CHART

Subgroups Included: ______________________

Sum of Averages = S =

Number of Subgroups = K =

Grand Average = $\bar{\bar{X}} = \frac{S}{K}$ = __________ = [ ]

A_2 factor =

$UCL_{\bar{X}} = \bar{\bar{X}} + A_2\bar{R}$ =   + (   )(   ) = [ ]

$LCL_{\bar{X}} = \bar{\bar{X}} - A_2\bar{R}$ =   − (   )(   ) = [ ]

FACTORS FOR CONTROL LIMITS

n	d_2	D_3	D_4	A_2	$\tilde{A}_2$
2	1.128	0	3.267	1.880	1.880
3	1.693	0	2.575	1.023	1.187
4	2.059	0	2.282	0.729	0.796
5	2.326	0	2.115	0.577	0.691
6	2.534	0	2.004	0.483	0.548
7	2.704	.076	1.924	0.419	0.508
8	2.847	.136	1.864	0.373	0.433
9	2.970	.184	1.816	0.337	0.412
10	3.078	.223	1.777	0.308	0.362

INFORMATION / EXERCISE

41. With the data chart form, you can tell at a glance the **pattern** your data is following simply by noting the location of averages and ranges on the chart and how they change as time passes. However, this information is of questionable value without some guidelines to help us; we need more organization of our data.

EXERCISE 41. No response.

42. Two very useful control chart guidelines are well known to you; $\bar{\bar{X}}$ (the grand average), and $\bar{R}$ (the average range). Compute these values for the 25 samples, check the answers in the exercise column, and draw a solid line across your charts at the computed points.

$$\bar{\bar{X}} = \sum_{i=1}^{K} \bar{X}_i / K$$

where K = Number of samples

$$\bar{R} = \sum_{i=1}^{K} R_i / K$$

Round answers to 1 decimal place.

EXERCISE 42. Find the following:

$$\bar{\bar{X}} = \sum_{i=1}^{25} \bar{X}_i / 25$$

$$= (2.8 + (-.8) + \ldots + .4 + 1.0)/25$$

$$\bar{R} = \sum_{i=1}^{25} R_i / 25$$

$$= (12 + 11 + \ldots + 17 + 8)/25$$

43. This is how your charts should now look.

EXERCISE 43. See completed charts at end of answer key.

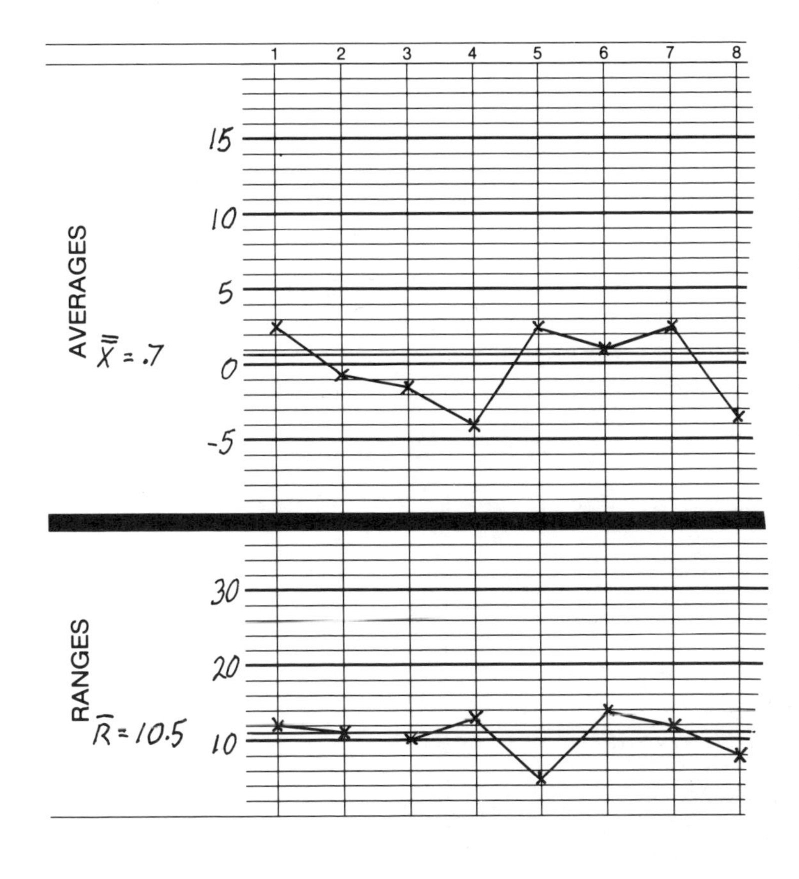

DATA

SAMPLE MEASUREMENTS	1	5	0	-8	-4	0
	2	8	-6	2	-8	3
	3	7	5	-3	-9	0
	4	-4	-3	1	4	5
	5	-2	0	2	-3	4
SUM		14	-4	-6	-20	12
AVERAGE, $\bar{X}$		2.8	-0.8	-1.2	-4.0	2.4
RANGE, R		12	11	10	13	5

INFORMATION

44. Since an average is a numerical measure of central tendency of a set of data, you expect to find some numbers above your $\bar{\bar{X}}$ line and some below it; the same applies to your $\bar{R}$ line.

45. If we assume there are no "unnatural" influences, we can say the probability of any one $\bar{X}$ falling on one side of the $\bar{\bar{X}}$ line is .5, or 50 percent (the .5 is a fraction, to convert any fraction to a percent just move the decimal point two places to the right). This simply means that, in the long run, we expect about half the values to be above the grand average and half below. (Certain exceptions will be discussed later.)

46. We now know the probability of getting any **one value** on one side of the $\bar{\bar{X}}$ or $\bar{R}$ lines. The probability of getting two (2) **consecutive** readings on one side of an average line is computed as follows:

PROBABILITY OF FIRST SAMPLE BEING ON ONE SIDE OF AVERAGE LINE = .5

PROBABILITY OF SECOND SAMPLE BEING ON ONE SIDE OF AVERAGE LINE = .5

PROBABILITY OF BOTH BEING ON THE SAME SIDE = PROBABILITY OF FIRST EVENT (P1) x PROBABILITY OF SECOND EVENT (P2) = .5 x .5 = .25.

47. This logic can be used to determine the probability of finding any number of consecutive samples on either side of an average line. A table of these probabilities would look like this:

Above or below average, consecutive readings	Probability
1	0.5
2	.25
3	.125
4	.0625
5	.03125
6	.0156
7	.0078
8	.0039
9	.00195
10	.00098

To put this table to work for you, all you need is an average line (either $\bar{\bar{X}}$ or $\bar{R}$). What you are looking for is something "unnatural" influencing your data. If you reviewed a chart and noticed six (6) consecutive readings above average, you could look at the above table and see that this would happen only 16 times in a thousand in a process with no unnatural influences (.016). What this means is that if you acted on the assumption that something (we call this something an "assignable cause of variation") was exerting an "undue" influence on your data, you would be wrong about 16 times in every thousand times you make this decision (i.e., there was really nothing influencing your data).

EXERCISE

44. In the first 25 samples, how many:

$\bar{X}$'s are above $\bar{\bar{X}}$? ____________________

$\bar{X}$'s below $\bar{\bar{X}}$? ____________________

R's above $\bar{R}$? ____________________

R's below $\bar{R}$? ____________________

45. In the long run, what fraction of our sample $\bar{X}$'s should be on one side of the $\bar{\bar{X}}$ line?

____

46. To find the probability of two events, you (circle one)

ADD

SUBTRACT

MULTIPLY

DIVIDE

the probabilities of each event, assuming the events aren't related to each other.

47. On the average, how many times in a thousand would you find seven (7) consecutive readings above an average even though there is no assignable cause influencing your data?

____

INFORMATION

48. The table on the preceding page is used to establish a "confidence" level. Determining the confidence level is simple enough:

$$\text{CONFIDENCE (in \%)} = (1-P) \times 100$$

where P = probability

A very common confidence level in control charting is the 99.0% level; this can be seen to be seven consecutive samples on either side of the average. Work it out as follows:

$$\begin{aligned}\text{CONFIDENCE} &= (1 - .0078) \times 100 \\ &= .992 \times 100 \\ &= 99.2 \text{ percent}\end{aligned}$$

(NOTE: Some companies act on a run of 8 instead of 7)

49. Obviously, you start getting pretty suspicious long before you reach the 99.0% confidence level. A common approach to this is to take samples more often when a "warning limit" is reached. A run of five (5) is suspicious enough to sample again immediately. If you have a touchy product, you may also wish to accept a lower confidence level. For example, you might decide to act on a run of six (6), and you would still have a confidence of 98.4 percent in your decision. (And, after all, nobody's perfect!) You can also make your chart more sensitive to change by taking larger samples.

50. Now that you've seen how useful just the average lines can be in evaluating charted data, you'll be excited to find that we're going to plot more lines on the charts! The other lines are known as "CONTROL LIMITS".

51. When using control limits, we must consider the $\overline{X}$ and R charts separately; even though $\overline{R}$ is used to find all limit lines.

52. Before getting into computing control limits, an explanation of the principle behind them is in order.

The principle governing the distribution of points on the control charts is called the principle of the normal distribution. Basically, this principle states that in any group of characteristics determined by only "random" causes, there will be a distinct distribution of frequencies, peaking at the average and falling off as you move further away from the average. The shape of this "frequency" distribution resembles a bell, and is often referred to as the "bell curve".

EXERCISE

48. What confidence level is a shop using if they act any time eight consecutive samples fall on either side of the average?

____

49. To get faster confirmation of a problem, you can:

   a. Take a bigger sample.

   b. Set a warning limit.

   c. Cut the tolerance.

Circle all that apply.

50. No response.

51. $\overline{R}$ is used only to find R chart lines.

____

True or False

52. The two factors needed to use the "Normal Table" are:

____

and ____________________________

INFORMATION

For our purposes here, the distribution can be described mathematically by the use of just two numbers and a table. One of the numbers is $\overline{X}$, a number you're familiar with. The other number is called "sigma", and the symbol for this is the lower-case Greek letter sigma, written σ. This value can be estimated from sample data by the following formula:

$$\sigma = \sqrt{\frac{\sum_{i=1}^{n} (X_i - \overline{X})^2}{n - 1}}$$

Many books have forms which can aid you in using this formula for computing σ; however, a much simpler way of estimating σ is available using $\overline{R}$ and we will show you how to use this formula later on (after we've described some precautions).

What the normal distribution says (in terms useful in QC) is that in a "random cause system" the expected frequencies of $\overline{X}$'s, or averages, will be symmetrical about the grand average, and 99.7 percent of all individuals will be within $\overline{\overline{X}} + 3\sigma$ and $\overline{\overline{X}} - 3\sigma$. Graphically, this is how the normal curve looks:

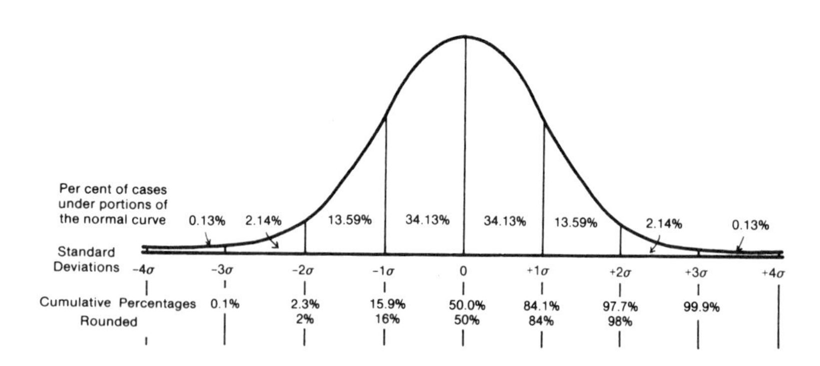

It would pay for you to study the graphic illustration. It says, in effect, that 68 percent of the items (which can be parts, pH readings, flow, sizes, etc.) will fall in the range from $\overline{\overline{X}}$ plus 1σ to $\overline{\overline{X}}$ minus 1σ; 95 percent of the items will be between $\overline{\overline{X}}$ plus 2σ and $\overline{\overline{X}}$ minus 2σ; and 99.7 percent of the items will be between $\overline{\overline{X}}$ plus 3σ and $\overline{\overline{X}}$ minus 3σ. In fact, tables exist (See Appendix, Table V or VIII) that allow you to determine with high precision what proportion of any normally distributed large population lies below or above any point, or between any two points. All you need to use the table is an estimate of $\overline{\overline{X}}$ and σ; you will learn how to do this later in this course.

53. The basic unit used in computing all control limits is $\overline{R}$. This factor is related to σ and, like σ, is a measure of **dispersion.**

54. Before we get into too much detail, a definition should be understood. "Control Limits" on an X bar chart are values computed from estimates of dispersion and are located symmetrically about the grand average.

EXERCISE

53. Two measures of dispersion are sigma (σ) and

____

54. Control limits are plotted without regard to the grand average.

____

True or False

INFORMATION

55. (The discussion below shows how to find statistical limits for range charts. A worksheet for placing limits on both X Bar and range charts is given on page 10.)

It is also possible to compute a "limit" for the range chart beyond which no value of R should fall. We call this a "control limit".

Actually, there are two control limits, an upper and a lower. To find the lower control limit for the range chart, just multiply the computed value of $\bar{R}$ by the D_3 factor given in the table below.

Sample size	D_3
2	0
3	0
4	0
5	0
6	0
7	.076
8	.136
9	.184
10	.223

If you check back to the data in Frame 40, you will see we used samples of 5; the corresponding value of D_3 is 0. Therefore, your lower control limit for R (from here out abbreviated LCL_R) is:

$$LCL_R = \bar{R}\,(D_3) = 10.5\,(0) = 0$$

Values of (D_3) for sample sizes from 2 to 25 are given in Table II of the appendix. Notice that for sample sizes below 7, the value is always 0.

56. The Upper Control Limit for ranges (abbreviated UCL_R) is computed in the same way as the lower control limit except that the table given factor now is D_4.

Sample size	D_4
2	3.267
3	2.574
4	2.282
5	2.114
6	2.004
7	1.924
8	1.864
9	1.816
10	1.777

We will use the following notation when discussing the X Bar Chart:

$LCL_{\bar{X}}$ = The Lower Control Limit for the X Bar Chart.

$UCL_{\bar{X}}$ = The Upper Control Limit for the X Bar Chart.

EXERCISE

55. The R chart has how many control limits?

____

The abbreviation for the lower control limit for ranges is:

____

To compute LCL_R, multiply the value

__________ by the factor __________.

56. The **method** for computing UCL_R is

— the same as

— different than

the method for computing LCL_R.

INFORMATION

EXERCISE

The Control Limits (both upper and lower) for the X Bar charts utilize A_2 factors. A brief table is shown here:

Sample size	A_2
2	1.880
3	1.023
4	0.729
5	0.577
6	0.483
7	0.419
8	0.373
9	0.337
10	0.308

A more complete table is Table II in the Appendix.

The control limits are computed using the formulas:

$LCL_{\overline{X}} = \overline{\overline{X}} - A_2\overline{R}$

$UCL_{\overline{X}} = \overline{\overline{X}} + A_2\overline{R}$

Using the data in frame 40, for samples of 5 we get $A_2 = 0.577$. The values of $\overline{\overline{X}}$ and $\overline{R}$ for this data were computed in Frame 42. Thus

$LCL_{\overline{X}} = .7 - (.577)(10.5) = -5.3585$ or approximately -5.4

$UCL_{\overline{X}} = .7 + (.577)(10.5) = 6.7575$ or approximately 6.8

Again, the upper control limit for the range chart is computed by multiplying the table factor of D_4 for your sample size of 5 by the value of $\overline{R}$, or

$UCL_R = \overline{R}\ (D_4) = 10.5\ (2.114) = 22.197$ or approximately 22.2

The values given on the chart in the answer key were obtained **without** rounding off any values.

57. The control limit line is shown on the chart as a broken line, as shown below.

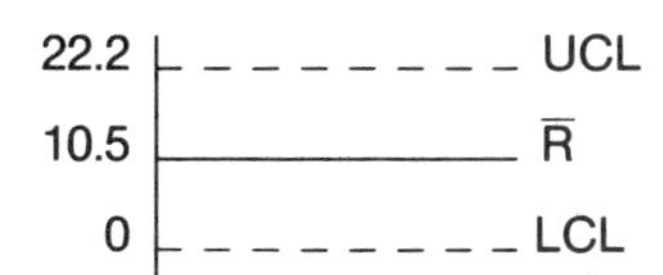

The control limit iine is

— solid

— broken

58. You now have three lines on your R chart, the LCL (which is zero), the UCL, and $\overline{R}$. The relationship between these lines and the values of R for each sample can be analyzed statistically.

No response.

59. Refer to the figure in Frame 52. The R chart is based on an approximation of the normal distribution, which is shown graphically in Frame 52. For QC purposes (though not **precisely correct**) the following assumptions can be made:

$\overline{R}$ is equivalent to $\overline{\overline{X}}$

LCL_R is equavalent to $\overline{\overline{X}} - 3\sigma$

UCL_R is equivalent to $\overline{\overline{X}} + 3\sigma$

59. For QC purposes, the UCL_R can be considered equivalent to the value

____

INFORMATION

60. When you evaluate **any** control chart, you are actually posing a question, namely:

    Does the charted data indicate a lack of control?

    In quality control evaluation, you normally give the process the benefit of the doubt; you only answer the question "yes" if you are at least 99 percent sure of yourself. This is the confidence level which was referred to in Frame 48—you may wish to review this concept.

EXERCISE

60. Control charts are evaluated at the ______ percent confidence level.

---

61. You will find it best to define "control" as the absence of variation which can be traced to a specific cause. In other words, control can be defined as a situation where only **random** variation is present. This concept causes much confusion, but it is important that you understand it.

61. In a controlled process, only __________ variation is present.

---

62. So, in effect, when you approach a process that is "control charted", you are posing the question:

    CAN I SAY WITH 99 PERCENT CONFIDENCE THAT THE VARIATION IN THIS PROCESS IS NOT RANDOM?

    The above question can be answered "yes" according to the rules that follow.

62. No response.

---

63. You've already learned (see frame 48) that you can answer the question "yes" if there are seven consecutive readings on one side of the average line (this confidence level does not apply to range charts if the subgroup size is less than three (3), preferably five (5) or more).

63. A process is deemed out of control if ______________ consecutive readings are on one side of the average line.

---

64. We also know that in a controlled process, 99.7 percent of all readings will be below $\bar{\bar{X}} + 3\sigma$; our UCL_R corresponds to this value. Therefore, you can answer the question yes if **any** value of R exceeds the UCL_R.

64. A **single** point beyond the control limit indicates a problem with the process.

    ____

    True or False

---

65. Mentally divide each half of the control chart (a half control chart is the distance from the average to either control limit) into thirds and consider the distribution of points in each third. Again, your guide to evaluating the chart is the normal distribution.

    To begin, consider **only one half** of the control chart at a time.

65. In analyzing a control chart, you begin with the entire chart.

    ____

    True or False

---

66. Consider the diagram in the exercise column. You see that the mental division of the half chart into thirds is the equivalent of dividing a normal distribution at (+ or −) one and two standard deviations. Since our control chart distribution is hypothetically a normal distribution, we expect our charted points to follow the approximate pattern of a normal distribution. Thus, we can expect approximately one third (34 percent) of our points to fall in the third of the chart from the average (either $\bar{\bar{X}}$ or $\bar{R}$) to one standard deviation, about one point in every seven should fall between one and two standard deviations, and about one point in every forty should fall between two and three standard deviations—the outer third of your "half chart".

66.

3σ	
	zone c (1 in 40)
2σ	
	zone b (1 in 7)
1σ	
	zone a (1 in 3)
avg.	

INFORMATION	EXERCISE
67. The above information will help you "scan" a control chart for unnatural trends or groupings—or the lack of expected groupings. Once a suspicious set of data points is discovered, you will want to "test your hypothesis" that the suspicious data indicates a lack of control at the 99 percent confidence level.	67. In the analysis of control charts, you should scan the data, looking for: ______________ or ______________.
68. For samples of 5 (which is recommended) analysis of $\overline{X}$ and R charts can be the same without losing too much accuracy. The rules given below are based on samples of five; for samples smaller than five, the analysis may not hold for the R chart, though $\overline{X}$ chart analysis can be applied regardless of sample size.	68. Analysis of both $\overline{X}$ and R charts can be the same for samples of ______________. For smaller samples, R chart analysis is different.
69. A review of the normal distribution is in order. See Frame 52 and Table V of the appendix.	69. What is the cumulative percent below $\overline{\overline{X}} + 2\sigma$? ______________ $\overline{\overline{X}} - 2\sigma$? ______________
70. You will recall from Frame 46 that we found the probability of getting a certain number of consecutive points on one side of the average by multiplying the probability of an event by the probability of all preceding events. This simple process is the same one we will use now to establish your "confidence limit" of 99 percent for other unnatural distributions.	70. No response.
71. Consider your process out of control if you find two (2) out of three (3) consecutive points fall above the $+2\sigma$ line or below the -2σ lines (Zone C). The probability of this happening in a controlled process is computed by taking the probability of one point falling in Zone C (.0227) times the probability of a point not falling in Zone C (1 - .0227 = .9773), times the probability of another point in Zone C, times 3 (since any of the three points might be outside of Zone C); thus, we find the odds of two out of three points falling in Zone C (again, you must consider only half the chart at a time in this analysis) is: $3 \times .0227 \times .0227 \times .9773 = .0015$ and your confidence level is: $1 - .0015 = .9985 = 99.85\%$	71. You can consider a process out of control if ______________ out of ______________ consecutive points fall in Zone ________. Zone C represents the area between ______________σ and ______________σ.
72. Consider your process out of control if you find four out of five consecutive points above the $+1\sigma$ line or below the -1σ line (Zone B or beyond). Probability of one point in Zone B or beyond = .1586. You then take this figure times itself four times (**four** of five consecutive points): $.1586 \times .1586 \times .1586 \times .1586 = .00063$	72. You can consider a process out of control if 4 of 5 consecutive points are in Zone ____ or beyond.

INFORMATION

This is the probability of getting four points **in a row** in Zone B or beyond. To find the probability of getting four of **five** consecutive points in Zone B or above, you must multiply this figure by the probability of getting one point outside of Zone B or beyond, which is 1 - .1586 = .8414, and multiply this product by 5. The whole operation goes like this:

Probability of 4 out of 5 in Zone B or beyond:

$.1586 \times .1586 \times .1586 \times .1586 \times .8414 \times 5 = .0027$

and your confidence level is:

$1 - .0027 = .9973 = 99.73\%$

73. To summarize, you can say with high confidence that your process is out of control if any of the following conditions occur:

- Seven consecutive points fall on the same side of the average (Zone A or beyond).
- Four out of five consecutive points fall in Zone B or beyond.
- Two out of three consecutive points in Zone C or beyond.
- Any single point beyond Zone C (above your upper control limit or below your lower control limit).

You also know how these figures are arrived at and can therefore adjust the "tests" and confidence levels to suit your own special needs. For example, many companies use a run of 8 in Zone A or beyond instead of 7.

Remember that when you use the tests described above, you consider only half of the chart at once.

74. In addition to the "half chart analysis", there are tests you can make that involve considering the entire chart at once.

75. One such test is a test for stratification. To find out if your sampling data is stratified, you consider the number of consecutive points in Zone A. Although you know most of your data points (68 percent) should fall in Zone A, you also recognize that some points (32 percent) should fall outside of this zone; if this doesn't happen, you say your data is "stratified". You compute the number of consecutive readings you can tolerate in Zone A in the same way you computed your half chart tests. It turns out you can consider thirteen consecutive points in Zone A as evidence of stratification at the 99 percent level of confidence; specifically:

$.6826^{13} = .007$ (means ".6826 to the 13th power", or times itself 13 times).

Your confidence level is:

$1 - .007 = .993 = 99.3\%$

EXERCISES

74. Some analysis involves considering the entire control chart at once.

____

True or False

75. How many consecutive points can be allowed in Zone A?

____

INFORMATION

76. Obviously, we can find the opposite of the above situation also—that is, an absence of points in Zone A. Often you will pick up these conditions in your half chart study. However, there is a chance that the points might fluctuate from zone to zone in such a manner that the situation will become apparent sooner in an analysis of the entire chart for "mix." To discover abnormal mix, you observe the number of consecutive points falling outside of Zone A. The probability of any one point falling outside of Zone A is .3174. You can consider your data out of control if you find five (5) consecutive points outside of Zone A.

    This is computed as follows:

    $.3174 \times .3174 \times .3174 \times .3174 \times .3174 = .3174^5 = .0032$

    And your confidence level is:

    $1 - .0032 = .9968 = 99.68\%$

77. Most people involved in the control of quality deal with tolerances, and for control charts to be truly useful, they must be related to tolerances. Up to now, we have concentrated on **Process Control** and not considered the tolerances. It is important that it be done in this way in the real world application of control charts—that is, to concentrate initial efforts on process control. The steps involved in this are:

    1. Gather sample data from the process and plot on $\overline{X}$ and R charts.
    2. After twenty or more samples are drawn, compute $\overline{\overline{X}}$, $\overline{R}$, and control limits for the $\overline{X}$ and R charts.
    3. Analyze the charts; if assignable causes are apparent take action to remove the suspected causes and return to step one.
    4. Perform steps 1 through 3 until at least 25 consecutive samples are "in control" by all the analyses we have studied. **At this point,** you can begin to consider the relationship of the process and the tolerance.

    These four steps and the subsequent comparison with tolerances are **elements** in a Process Capability Study.

78. The reason comparison of the processes with the tolerance is delayed until the process is brought into control is that until this point is reached, the process is unpredicatble and there is very little you can say about this process with a high level of confidence.

79. Many pages back, we promised you would learn a simple way to compute σ, using $\overline{R}$. This can be done ONLY IF YOUR PROCESS IS IN CONTROL! Remember, control is no longer a vague concept to you; it is very explicitly defined as the absence of reaction to any of your tests for abnormal data distribution (see Frames 67 through 73) on either the $\overline{X}$ or R chart for at least 25 consecutive samples.

EXERCISES

76. How many consecutive points can be allowed to fall beyond Zone A?

    ____

77. The steps in Frame #77 describe what?

    ____

78. An out-of-control process is:

    ____

79. If the process is in control:

    $\sigma = \overline{R}/$ ____________________

INFORMATION

When this controlled condition exists, the following relationship holds true:

$$\sigma = \overline{R}/d_2$$

The factor d_2 varies with the sample size, and Table II gives the value of d_2 for various samples sizes, see the Appendix. A brief table is included with the worksheet after Frame 40.

80. Once the value of σ is known, the capability of the process can be determined. We know that 99.7 percent of the parts will be between $\overline{\overline{X}} - 3\sigma$, and $\overline{\overline{X}} + 3\sigma$, so to be considered "capable" of producing nearly all parts within the limits of the tolerance, the tolerance must be AT LEAST 6σ wide. And, since we expect some drifting of the average, we must allow some leeway for small changes in the process average.

Methods of defining process capability are as varied as the Quality Engineers making the definition. Two methods are given below—either will serve you well.

Describing Process Capability

Method 1: Classify Process as Acceptable or Unacceptable based on the following rules.

Acceptable if 6σ is equal to or less than 75 percent of the tolerance.

Formula: Accept if tolerance/6 $(\overline{R}/d_2)$ is 1.33 or greater. (Note: This ratio is sometimes called the C_P index. Some companies require their suppliers to have C_P indexes of at least 1.)

Method 2: Classify Process based on Ratio of Process Spread to Tolerance—the "Capability Ratio"

Formula: $$\text{Capability Ratio} = \frac{\text{Tolerance}}{(\overline{R}/d_2)}$$

(Note that this is just 6 times C_P.)

Significance of Capability Ratio:

Less than 8.0—Process not capable of meeting tolerance.

From 8.0-10.0—Marginal (but acceptable) capability. Monitor with $\overline{X}$ and R charts, samples of 5 or larger.

From 10.0-20.0—Capable process. Monitor with $\overline{X}$ and R charts, runs charts, or median charts (see next section).

Over 20—Extremely capable process. Monitor on an audit basis only.

EXERCISES

80. Using Method 2, you compute a capability ratio of 6.0; is the process capable of meeting tolerance?

____

INFORMATION

81. The $\overline{X}$ and R charts have had many successful applications in industry, and probably many more applications as yet untried. The background you've obtained from this course up to now should enable you to successfully set up and interpret $\overline{X}$ and R charts. Please keep in mind, however, that this **technical knowhow** must be tempered by your good judgment in engineering, management, and economics. Use your common sense.

$\overline{X}$ and R charts used together as instruments to organize and present data for evaluation are valuable tools. Start your program properly (see Frame #77), administer it wisely, and the payoff of improved quality, lower failure costs, and enhanced productivity will make the logic of the program obvious.

Keep in mind that **constant improvement** is the goal of quality control. After a stable process has been obtained you should continue to evaluate the process data to see if it has improved. If so you should search for the cause of the **improvement** just as hard as you would seek the cause of a **problem.** Only by doing this can you stay ahead of your competitor—and keep your customer satisfied.

EXERCISE

81. The goal of quality control is to achieve stability, and to then maintain this level.

____

True or False

Control Charts for Averages and Ranges
ANSWER KEY

FRAME	ANSWER
1	Quality Control
2	Programmed instruction
4	No correct: 12.10 15.75 3256.20
5	Divide top number by bottom number
7	.25
8	.348, .347, .255, .7
9	4, 3, 5
11	2.1, 210, 2100, .21, .021
12	$221\overline{)150}$ = .6787 $1555\overline{)1555}$ = 1 $210\overline{)21.0}$ = .1
13	Code values
14	1.004 = +4, 1.003 = +3, .997 = −3, .995 = − 5
16	Negative
17	10 degrees
18	− 5 is below zero, 8 is above zero
19	5, 2, 8, 2, 1, 4, 4, 3
20	10, 9, 8
21	Range
22	9, 15, 9
23	.007, .005, .003
24	x
25	R
26	−1.2, 1.0, −4.0, 4.0
27	Negative
28	X bar
29	$\overline{R}$, "R bar"
30	False
31	No
32	Formula
33	Σ
34	$\overline{X}_A = O_A + (\overline{X}_c)(i)$ $.998 = 1.000 + (-2.0)(.001)$
35	2, 2, −1, −1
36	−18, 0, 1, 1, 0, 1, −1, −1

FRAME	ANSWER
38	Graph
42	$\overline{\overline{X}} = 17.4/25 = .696$ $\overline{R} = 262/25 = 10.48$
44	$\overline{X}$'s: 16 above, 9 below R's: 14 above, 11 below
45	½
46	Multiply
47	8
48	(1 − .0039) x 100 = 99.6%
49	a or b
51	False
52	$\overline{\overline{X}}$ and σ
53	$\overline{R}$
54	False
55	2 control limits, LCL_R Multiply $\overline{R}$ by D_3
56	Same as
57	Broken
59	$\overline{X} + 3\sigma$
60	99
61	Random
63	7
64	True
65	False
67	Trends or groupings
68	5 or more
69	97.7%, 2.3%
71	2 out of 3 in zone C. 2σ and 3σ.
72	B
74	True
75	12 or less
76	4 or less
77	A process capability study
78	Unpredictable
79	d_2
80	No, any drift would cause rejects.
81	False. The goal is improvement.

Quality America, Inc.®

ANSWER KEY
CONTROL CHARTS FOR AVERAGES AND RANGES

PART NAME	DIMENSION CHARTED	ZERO VALUE	CLASS INTERVAL
		0	1

PART NUMBER	START DATE	END DATE	UCL AVERAGES	$\bar{\bar{X}}$	LCL AVERAGES	R BAR	UCL RANGES
			6.7430	.6960	-5.3510	10.48	22.1652

SAMPLE MEASUREMENTS																										
	1	5	0	-8	-4	0	-6	8	1	7	4	1	-1	-5	4	-4	0	-3	-2	-4	4	2	-9	-1	2	3
	2	8	-6	2	-8	3	-3	-4	-7	1	4	0	0	4	9	8	5	-7	3	5	6	4	-8	0	-2	4
	3	7	5	-3	-9	0	1	4	-7	9	3	-1	-2	-4	0	-2	-1	-1	8	4	6	4	9	-5	9	0
	4	-4	-3	1	4	5	8	1	-2	-4	1	0	8	2	0	-5	1	3	-3	0	2	1	0	-8	1	-4
	5	-2	0	2	-3	4	5	4	-3	-6	-1	5	4	7	6	-6	1	5	5	8	0	0	0	4	-8	2
SUM		14	-4	-6	-20	12	5	13	-18	7	11	5	9	4	19	-9	+6	-3	11	13	18	11	-8	-10	2	5
AVERAGE, $\bar{X}$		2.8	-.8	-1.2	-4	2.4	1	2.6	-3.6	1.4	2.2	1	1.8	.8	3.8	-1.8	1.2	-.6	2.2	2.6	3.6	2.2	-1.6	-2	.4	1
RANGE, R		12	11	10	13	5	14	12	8	15	5	6	10	12	9	14	6	12	11	12	6	4	18	12	17	8
		1	2	3	4	5	6	7	8	9	10	11	12	13	14	15	16	17	18	19	20	21	22	23	24	25

AVERAGES

15
10
6.7430
5
.6960 0
-5.3510 -5

RANGES

30
22.1652
20
10.4800 10

CONTROL CHARTS FOR INDIVIDUAL MEASUREMENTS
and
OTHER VARIABLES CHARTS

CONTROL CHARTS FOR INDIVIDUAL MEASUREMENTS
and
OTHER VARIABLES CHARTS

CONTROL CHARTS FOR INDIVIDUALS

While the $\overline{X}$ and R charts are the most sensitive, accurate, and "desirable" control charts, they are by no means the only control charts available. In many situations, you may find it advantageous to use some other control charts. The remaining sections will enable you to establish, as part of your program, several other important types of charts, including:

Other Variable Charts (for "Measurable" Characteristics)

— Control Charts for Individual Pieces (or Measurements)
— Runs Charts
— Median Charts

Attribute Control Charts

– For Percent Defective (p Charts)
– For Number of Defectives (np Charts)
– For Number of Defects per Unit (c charts)

It is virtually certain that you will encounter applications for one or several of these charts—so stay with it; you're well on your way to control chart mastery!

INFORMATION

1. $\overline{X}$ and R chart interpretation assumes the data should follow a "normal" bell-shaped distribution, and since we are plotting averages, this is a safe assumption because AVERAGES ARE ALWAYS NEARLY NORMALLY DISTRIBUTED.

   For example, if you rolled a single die and recorded the numbers as they came up, you would eventually end up with a chart that looked a lot like this:

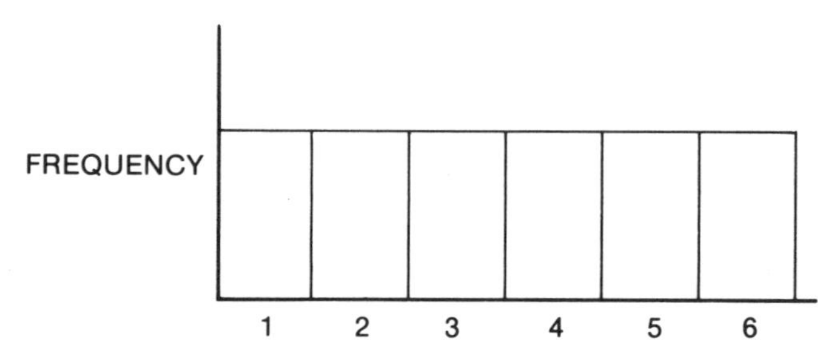

   In other words, the numbers would come up in nearly equal frequencies.

   Now, if you rolled two dice and recorded the totals, you would get a frequency distribution that looked something like this:

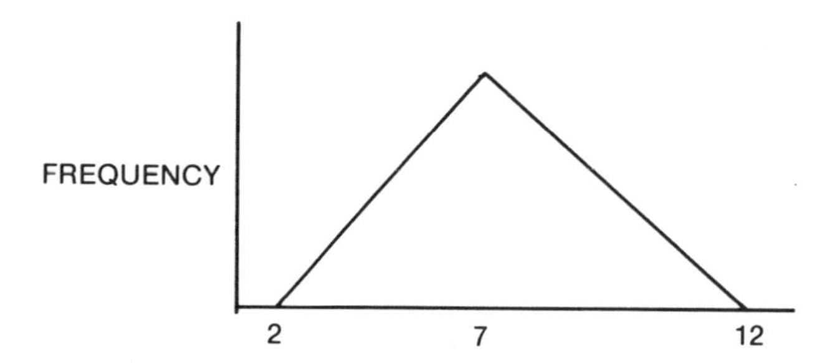

EXERCISES

1. Averages are nearly always ____________ distributed.

INFORMATION

EXERCISES

Notice that this is much closer to the bell curve than the first chart. As you added more dice, your distribution would look like this:

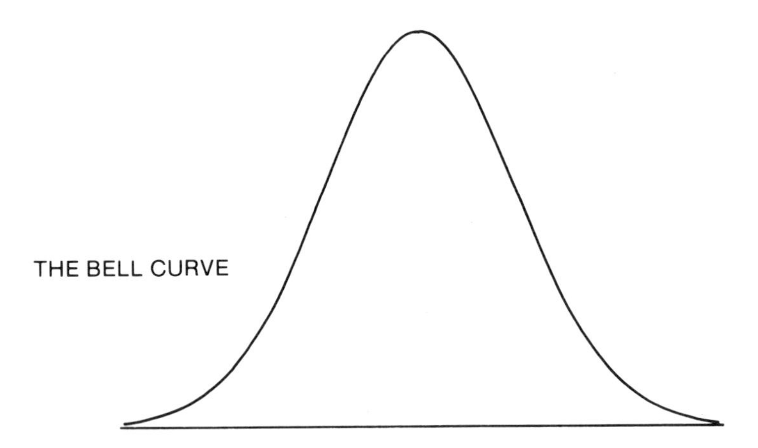

If you consider each die as a random variable, you can see that the more random variables you have influencing a result, the better your chance of having a normally distributed variable measurement. With the $\overline{X}$ chart, we've been quite safe in assuming that our data should be normally distributed.

2. However, if we choose to plot on a chart the individual measurements instead of averages, we must study the distribution of the individual readings to see if it appears to be a normal distribution. While there are many ways of doing this, most are too involved for our purposes here—you are urged to consult some of the many fine texts available on quality control or statistics.

   A simple test of normality is a visual "goodness to fit" test. To conduct this test, you perform the following steps.

   — Collect a number of measurements (about 130) in groups of five. Plot on a control chart.

   — Compute σ and $\overline{X}$ using the formulas learned in the previous section (see frames 42, 52 and 79).

   — Plot the measurements on a histogram.

   — Compute the expected frequency in each cell and draw a line through the points on your histogram.

   — Compare the "theorectical curve" with your real data histogram. If, in your judgment, the two distributions are close enough, then conclude the data is normally distributed.

   Note: The process control chart **must** be in control before performing this goodness of fit test!

3. Let's step through a goodness-to-fit test together.

   Step 1: Collect a number of measurements. Code values read as follows (we're using 70; in practice you'll use 130 or more):

5	0	-3	3	0	1	-2
1	0	-2	0	0	1	4
-1	2	1	-1	0	-1	-2
0	-1	0	-1	1	-1	0
0	1	0	2	1	-1	1

INFORMATION

EXERCISES

1	1	1	0	-2	0	1
-6	0	1	0	2	1	0
3	0	2	1	0	1	1
0	0	-2	-1	0	-2	1
0	-3	-2	0	1	0	3

Step 2: Compute $\overline{X}$ and σ

$\sigma = (\overline{R}/d_2) = (\Sigma R/K)/d_2 = (55/14)/2.326$
$= 3.9/2.326 = 1.69$

$\overline{X} = \Sigma X/n = 11/70 = .16$

Step 3: Plot the measurements on a Histogram. An example of a histogram is shown below.

HISTOGRAM

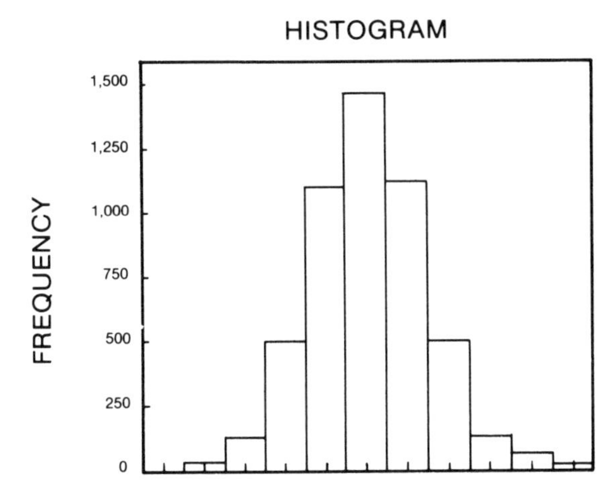

Step 4: Compute the expected frequency at each code value and draw a line through the points on your histogram.

The "expected frequency" at each code value is the frequency given in tables V and VIII, Areas under the normal curve. Notice the table is indexed in Z values. The Z value is obtained by subtracting $\overline{X}$ from the value you are concerned about (X_i) and dividing the answer by σ.

In our case, we want to know first of all how many units are between $\overline{X}$ and +1. The answer is found by subtracting $\overline{X}$ from +1 (1 - .16 = .84) and dividing this by σ, which gives .84/1.69 = .50. Therefore, Z = 0.50.

Notice that table VIII gives the areas between $\overline{X}$ and your value X_i. This is what we are looking for! We simply go down the left-hand column until we find 0.5, then over to the right until you are in the column whose number matches the second decimal place of your Z number; in this case, zero. Here we find the number .19146. (Assume there is a decimal point in front of all the numbers in the table.)

z	0.00	0.01
0.0	00000	00399
0.1	03983	04380
0.2	07926	08317
0.3	11791	12172
0.4	15554	15910
0.5	19146	19497

INFORMATION

EXERCISES

The number represents the proportion of a normal population expected to fall between $\overline{X}$ and $+0.5\sigma = Z$. Since we checked 70 parts, we expect to find 70 times .19146 parts between .16 and +1, or 13.4 parts. Mark a point on your histogram midway between .16 and +1 at a frequency of 13.4 (see figure).

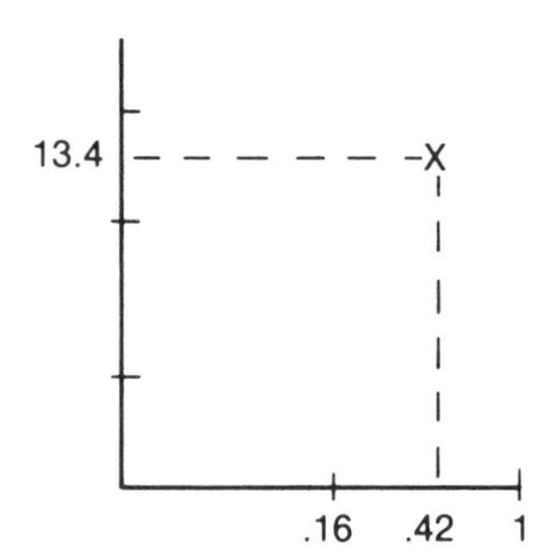

The number expected between +1 and +2 is computed in a similar manner. First you find the proportion between $\overline{X}$ and the smaller value, then between $\overline{X}$ and the larger value; then just subtract to find the difference. In our case,

PROPORTION BETWEEN $\overline{X}$ AND +1 = .19146

PROPORTION BETWEEN $\overline{X}$ AND +2: $\frac{2 - .16}{1.69} = Z = 1.09$

PROPORTION CORRESPONDING TO Z of 1.09 = .36214

PROPORTION BETWEEN +1 and +2 IS
.36214 − .19146 = .17068

This value times our sample size of 70 gives us our frequency between +1 and +2, or Fe = 70 (.17068) = 11.9. We will use Fe to represent the expected frequency.

This point is marked in the appropriate place on the histogram. Complete the plotting for the other code values on the positive side of $\overline{X}$.

Z numbers on the negative side of $\overline{X}$ are computed in exactly the same way. Be very careful to observe the rules for math using negative numbers covered earlier in this book. Just for illustration, we'll walk through an example. The Z value for the zone between $\overline{X}$ and -1 code value is:

$$\frac{X_i - \overline{X}}{\sigma} = \frac{-1 - (+.16)}{1.69} = Z = -.69$$

The negative sign can be ignored here, but it does serve notice that your value X_i and the frequency corresponding to it falls below the average.

The proportion of parts corresponding to Z = 0.69 is .25490, or 17.8 pieces in our sample.

Complete the plotting for the negative side of the histogram.

INFORMATION

EXERCISES

The completed "curve" fitted to the histogram is shown below.

Histogram vs. Normal Curve

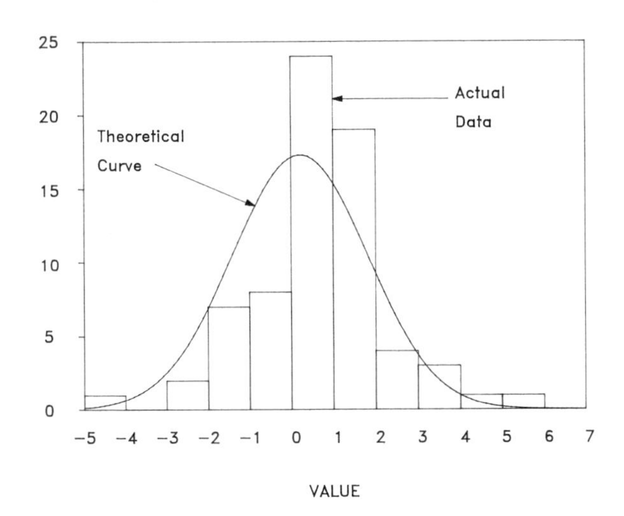

RANGE	EXPECTED FREQUENCY(*)	OBSERVED FREQUENCY
below −5	.08	1
−5 to −4	.4	0
−4 to −3	1.7	0
−3 to −2	4.9	2
−2 to −1	10.2	7
−1 to 0	15.1	8
0 to +1	16.0	24
1 to 2	11.9	19
2 to 3	6.4	4
3 to 4	2.4	3
4 to 5	.7	1
5 and above	.22	1

Note: −5 to −4 means −5 up to but not including −4.

If the general shape of the curve is approximately a match to the histogram, it is said to "fit". Variation is to be expected to some degree, since the curve is fitted for an infinite population and your data is only a sample. Generally, if your histogram is approximately bell shaped, you accept the hypothesis that the distribution is normal; since much variable data is normally distributed, this is generally safe.

INFORMATION

EXERCISES

4. Statisticians and engineers generally abhor "eyeball" judgments as just described. Fortunately, there is a relatively simple test called a Chi-Square goodness-to-fit test.

   This test yields a number that can be compared to a "critical value". A method of performing the Chi-Square (Symbolized χ^2) test is given below. The method assumes that you estimate the population mean and standard deviation by $\overline{X}$ and σ, respectively.

   If the computed value of χ^2 falls outside the critical region, you can say, with 95 percent confidence, that your data is **not** normally distributed.

   If you suspect the lack of normality is due to an assignable cause, you should take action to discover and remove the cause, then resample and retest.

$$\chi^2 = \Sigma \frac{(Fo - Fe)^2}{Fe}$$

Consider the population normally distributed unless χ^2 is greater than 7.81.

The way the value χ^2 is computed in the table is as follows.

Column 1: After computing $\overline{X}$ and σ, you are ready to determine the expected number in your population in each "cell" given in Column 1; always use this breakdown (6 cells) when using the "critical value" of 7.81.

Column 2: This is obtained from table VIII.

Column 3: The **proportion** in Column 2 (percentage divided by 100) for each cell times your sample size gives you the expected frequency.[1]

Column 5: Column 4 minus Column 3.

Column 6: Column 5 squared.

Column 7: Column 6 divided by Column 3.

The table for our sample data would look something like this:

χ^2 Test for Goodness of Fit

1	2	3	4	5	6	7
VALUES	NORMAL %	FREQ. EXPECTED	FREQ. OBSERVED	Fo - Fe	$(Fo - Fe)^2$	$\frac{(Fo - Fe)^2}{Fe}$
$+2\sigma$ or larger	2.28	1.60	2	.40	.16	.100
$+1\sigma$ to $+2\sigma$	13.59	9.51	7	-2.51	6.30	.662
$\overline{X}$ to $+1\sigma$	34.14	23.90	19	-4.90	24.01	1.005
$\overline{X}$ to -1σ	34.14	23.90	31	7.10	50.41	2.109
-1σ to -2σ	13.59	9.51	9	- .51	.260	.027
-2σ or smaller	2.28	1.60	1	- .60	.360	.225

1 Theorists recommend that Fe be at least three (3) in any cell. To obtain this, we need to check 130 parts.

INFORMATION

$$\chi^2 = \Sigma \frac{(Fo - Fe)^2}{Fe} = \Sigma(\text{Col } 7) = 4.128$$

$4.128 \leq 7.81$

Since the calculated value is within the critical region, we can't say the distribution is non-normal and will instead accept the hypothesis of normality.

5. Once you accept that your data is normally distributed, you can safely set up control charts for measurements from individual pieces. These charts are called X charts (not $\overline{X}$ charts).

6. The control limits for X charts still require that the values of $\overline{\overline{X}}$ and σ be computed. Since the process must be in control before σ can be computed from the value of $\overline{R}$, and since it is often best to use $\overline{X}$ and R charts in establishing process control, $\overline{X}$ and R charts often precede control charts for individual measurements. In fact, it is not unheard of to have machine operators keeping X charts while the Quality group simultaneously keeps $\overline{X}$ and R charts. ($\overline{X}$ and R charts are much more sensitive.)

7. The control limits for X charts are set at $\overline{\overline{X}} - 3\sigma$ and $\overline{\overline{X}} + 3\sigma$. If σ is computed from $\overline{R}$, be sure to group the data into samples of the same size and divide the average sample range $\overline{R}$ by the appropriate d_2 factor.

8. Once the $\overline{\overline{X}}$ line and the control limits are established, the individual measurements are plotted on the chart. The patterns that develop on the chart can be interpreted in **exactly the same way** as patterns on the $\overline{X}$ chart.

10. A logical question at this point is: What if our data isn't normally distributed, is there any quality procedure we can use? The answer is **YES.** There are many statistical methods that don't consider the underlying distribution of the data. These are called **Non-Parametric Statistical Methods.**

11. One particularly useful nonparametric tool is a "run chart". This is just a plot of the data set in the order in which the results were generated. A run chart usually has only a center line and no control limits.

12. When using run charts we use a different measure of central tendency than the grand average, $\overline{\overline{X}}$. The measure we use is the MEDIAN, symbolized $\tilde{X}$ the value which splits the data set into two equal groups. For example, if we have the values

EXERCISES

5. Control charts for individual measurements are called ______________ charts.

6. X charts and $\overline{X}$ and R charts always agree.

____
True or False

7. Control limits for X charts are set at

$\overline{\overline{X}} \pm$ ______________________

8. Interpretation of the X chart is

____
(Same/Different)

than the interpretation of $\overline{X}$ charts.

10. Before you can statistically analyze any data you must first determine the underlying distribution of the data.

____
True or False

11. A plot of fuel used week-by-week for a period of six months is called a

______________ ______________

12. Find the median of the following data sets

a) 8, 9, 1, 5, 1 ______________

b) 100.7, 78.5, 66.5 ______________

c) 56%, 30%, 75%, 56%, 20% ______________

INFORMATION

5
9
10
10 ← Median
11
20
21

then $\tilde{X} = 10$ since there are 3 values below and 3 above 10.

If the number of values is **odd** then the median value is always the middle value. Thus, the steps in finding the median for an odd number of values is

1. Put the data in rank order.
2. The middle value (found by counting) is $\tilde{X}$.

13. When the number of values is **even** the median is computed as midway between the two middle values. For example, if we have

6, 17, 155, 75

then we compute the median by putting the data in rank order

Rank	Value	
1	6	
2	17	Middle Values
3	75	Middle Values
4	155	

Then

$$\tilde{X} = \frac{75 + 17}{2} = 46$$

Notice there are 2 values above $\tilde{X}$ and 2 below $\tilde{X}$.

14. Once we have found $\tilde{X}$ we can test the hypothesis that the data came from a controlled process by analyzing runs on either side of the median.

First, let's look at the length of a run on the same side of $\tilde{X}$ which will lead us to conclude, at 99% confidence, that an assignable cause was present. This run length depends on the number of points plotted and is given in table X of the appendix.

An easy way to evaluate runs is to take the following steps.

1. Plot the data on a chart.
2. Count the total number of points.
3. Place a sheet of paper or a straight edge over the chart, covering the chart. Slide the paper slowly down the page, taking care to hold the edge parallel to the chart's horizontal axis.
4. When you have "exposed" half the total count above the edge of the paper to stop lowering the paper, you have found the median, $\tilde{X}$.
5. Draw a horizontal line at the median found.
6. Count the number of times the plotted line cuts across the median line. If a point is exactly on the line, count it so that you maximize your count (this has the effect of minimizing searches for assignable causes when none exist). If these are an odd number of cases, it may be necessary to disregard one value just equal to the median. If so, try to disregard a value that will not decrease the number of runs.

EXERCISES

13. Find the median of the following data sets:

a) 8°, 1°, 56°, 37°, 51°

b) $^{\$}5$, $^{\$}6$, $^{\$}156$

c) $180^{\#}$, $51^{\#}$, $31^{\#}$, $57^{\#}$

14. Plot a run chart for the following data and evaluate using runs above and below the median to test for an assignable cause.

YEAR	KENTUCKY DERBY WINNING TIME (coded)	NO.
1961	50	1
1962	12	2
1963	24	3
1964	10	4
1965	21	5
1966	30	6
1967	13	7
1968	31	8
1969	24	9
1970	42	10
1971	41	11
1972	24	12
1973	2	13
1974	50	14
1975	30	15
1976	23	16
1977	31	17
1978	21	18
1979	32	19
1980	30	20
1981	30	21
1982	32	22
1983	31	23

INFORMATION

7. Compare the count from step 6 to the minimum from table X. If your count is equal or greater than the table value then no assignable cause was acting on the process; otherwise an assignable cause should be looked for.

EXERCISE

Solution *(see run chart in answer key):*

The median is 30. There are

9 cases above 30
4 cases equal to 30
10 cases below 30

In order to use the total runs above and below the median as a test statistic we must add 1 median value to the "below" category, 2 to the "above" category, and disregard one median value. This should be done in a way that maximizes the number of runs. We accomplish this by calling the 1966 and 1981 cases "above," and the 1980 case "below," and disregarding the 1975 case.

After these assignments we find

8 runs above 30
7 runs below 30

15 total runs

We look in table X for 11 points below the median and find that at least 5 runs should be found. Since 15 is greater than 5 we see no indication of non-random influences (assignable causes).

15. If the data are truly random we expect the results to fluctuate above and below the median line in a random manner. The test in frame 14 is one way to check this. Another way would be to look for an abnormally long series of cases on the same side of the median. This test is very simple to apply.

    1. Perform steps 1-5 exactly the same as in frame 14.
    2. Find the largest run on either side of the median.
    3. Compare the length of this run to the maximum run length from table I.

    If the largest observed run is greater than the table value then conclude that an assignable cause was present.

15. Perform a run length test on the run chart from frame 14 to determine if an assignable cause was present.

16. Our final test for non-randomness will be to look for an unusually long series of increasing or decreasing values. If the number of consecutive increases or decreases exceeds the maximum in Table I we will conlude that something non-random is causing the increase or decrease.

16. Perform a test on the increases and decreases in the data from frame 14.

17. Another use for the median, other than that described above, is as a substitute for X Bar on control charts.

    Median charts, or $\tilde{X}$ charts (I call $\tilde{X}$ "X twiddle", but no one else does!), are not as sensitive as $\overline{X}$ charts but they offer the advantage of requiring **no calculations.**

    Of course to do this the group size must be an odd number, Also, the efficiency of the median versus the average drops so drastically for large samples that sample sizes less than 10 are strongly recommended. In practice, sample sizes are usually 3 or 5.

17. Medians can be found without using any calculations if the group size is

    ____

INFORMATION

18. In practice median charts are often used when there is resistance to computing averages. This may be because of time contraints or other reasons. The same reasons also make it necessary at times to drop the range chart and to keep only a median chart. However, you learned in the previous section that the range chart is necessary to control the **spread** of the process. A way of dealing with this is as follows:

   1. Use both a median and a range chart at first until both charts are in control.
   2. Once control is established, compute

   $$R_{MAX} = UCL_R - LCL_R$$

   Make a template of card stock as shown below

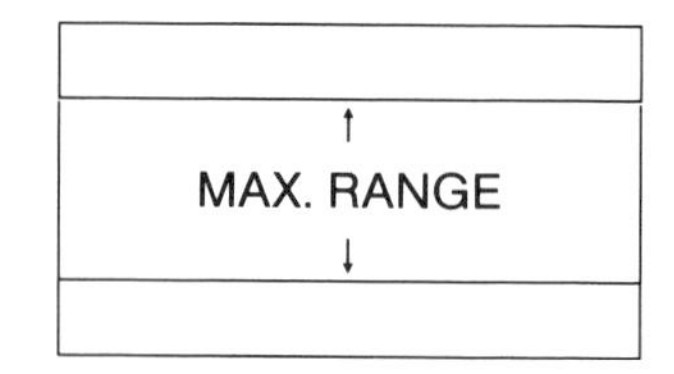

   3. Plot **all** the data on the chart — every measurement. Circle the median, e.g.

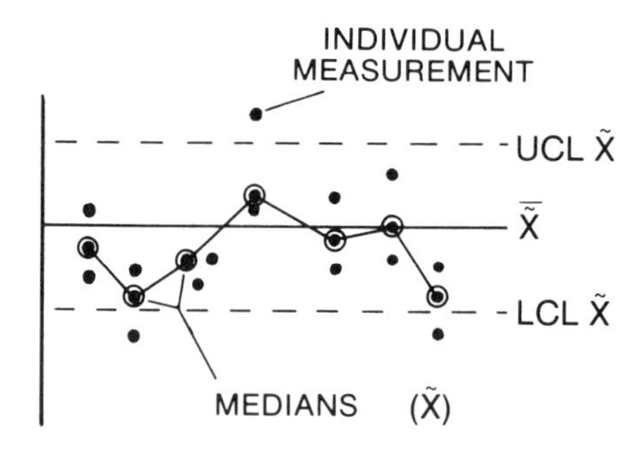

   4. Check the range by comparing the distance between the largest and smallest individual measurements to R_{MAX} using the template.

NOTE: The **medians,** not the individual values, are compared to the control limits.

EXERCISE

18. If no range chart is kept it is impossible to control the process spread.

____
True or False

INFORMATION

19. Control limits for median charts are computed in exactly the same way as for X bar charts except that the factor A_2 is replaced by $\tilde{A}_2$. $\tilde{A}_2$ factors are given on the worksheet after frame 1.41 and in Table II. The formulas for computing median chart control limits are

$$UCL_{\tilde{x}} = \overline{\tilde{X}} + \tilde{A}_2\overline{R}$$

$$LCL_{\tilde{x}} = \overline{\tilde{X}} - \tilde{A}_2\overline{R}$$

where

$UCL_{\tilde{x}}$ = upper control limit for medians

$LCL_{\tilde{x}}$ = lower control limit for medians

$\overline{\tilde{X}}$ = The average of the subgroup medians

$\tilde{A}_2$ and $\overline{R}$ have already been explained.

Please note that the X Bar worksheet can be used by simply replacing A_2 with $\tilde{A}_2$ in the formulas.

EXERCISE

19. Median chart control limits use the same equations as averages chart control limits except that ____________________
is replaced by ____________________.

Other Control Charts for Variables
ANSWER KEY

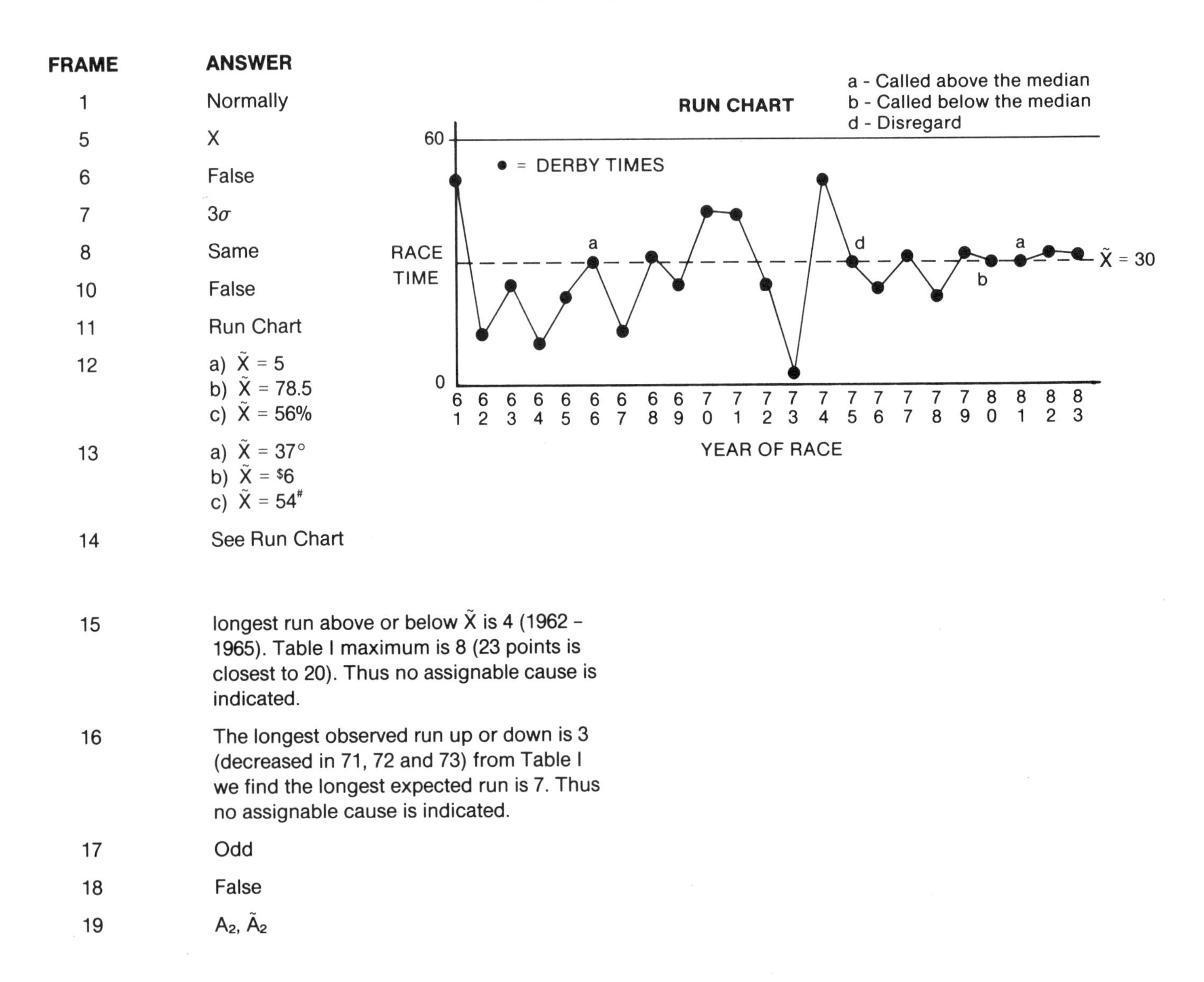

FRAME	ANSWER
1	Normally
5	X
6	False
7	3σ
8	Same
10	False
11	Run Chart
12	a) $\tilde{X} = 5$ b) $\tilde{X} = 78.5$ c) $\tilde{X} = 56\%$
13	a) $\tilde{X} = 37°$ b) $\tilde{X} = \$6$ c) $\tilde{X} = 54^{\#}$
14	See Run Chart
15	longest run above or below $\tilde{X}$ is 4 (1962 – 1965). Table I maximum is 8 (23 points is closest to 20). Thus no assignable cause is indicated.
16	The longest observed run up or down is 3 (decreased in 71, 72 and 73) from Table I we find the longest expected run is 7. Thus no assignable cause is indicated.
17	Odd
18	False
19	A_2, $\tilde{A}_2$

CONTROL CHARTS FOR ATTRIBUTES

CONTROL CHARTS FOR ATTRIBUTES

ATTRIBUTE CONTROL CHARTS

INFORMATION

1. While a variable characteristic can be measured and a number fixed to it, there are other characteristics that can only be described as "good" or "bad". These are termed ATTRIBUTE CHARACTERISTICS.

2. Some examples of attribute characteristics are:
   - Is there a leak or not?
   - Does the casting have porosity or not?
   - Is the fabric color right or not?
   - Will the shaft fit the ring gage or not?

   Notice that some of these characteristics **could** be measured as variables.

3. When inspecting for attributes, it is common to count the number of units possessing (or failing to posses) the attribute looked for; as well as the total number of units inspected. This information provides the basic data for several different control charts, these are charts for proportions defective in samples. The most common of these charts is the p chart.

4. You will often find that past inspection records contain enough data to begin your evaluation of the proportion defective at a given operation. The first thing you need to do with your data is compute the average proportion defective, symbolized $\bar{p}$ of course.

$$\bar{p} = \frac{\text{NUMBER DEFECTIVE}}{\text{NUMBER INSPECTED}}$$

5. If your inspection data covers an adequate period of time, long enough to include most of the significant variables, you may wish to determine if the process was "stable" during the period (if it is, you will define $\bar{p}$ as the process capability). The traditional method of examining data for stability involves computing the proportion standard deviation (σ_p).

$$\sigma_p = \sqrt{\frac{\bar{p}\,(1 - \bar{p})}{n}}$$

   For example, if $\bar{p} = .025$, $n = 50$

$$\sigma_p = \sqrt{\frac{.025\ (1 - .025)}{50}} = \sqrt{.0004875} = .022$$

   Control limits are set at $\bar{p} - 3\sigma_p$ and $\bar{p} + 3\sigma_p$. If a control limit is less than 0 it is equal to 0; if it is greater than 1 it is set equal to 1.

EXERCISE

1. Characteristics classed as good or bad are called ________________

2. Attribute characteristics can **never** be measured as variables.

   ____

   True or False

3. Charts which use the number of defective units and the number of units sampled as base data are control charts for

   ________________ defective.

4. $\bar{p}$ stands for:

   ____

   ____

   ____

5. σp means proportion ________________

INFORMATION	EXERCISE

INFORMATION

6. Whenever possible, the sample size is fixed, and the sample proportion p plotted. If the data is in control (i.e., no point beyond the control limit, random pattern inside control limits), we can conclude that the process capability is $\bar{p}$. If performance at this level is satisfactory (in terms of field problems, subsequent assembly and processing, scrap costs, etc.), the process will probably be charted with a fixed sample size (the size of the sample depends on many factors such as costs, criticality, and so on) for p. If it is **not** satisfactory, management action will be required.

EXERCISE

6. With regular p charts, the sample size is usually fixed.

____

True or False

INFORMATION

7. Table VI contains upper control limit values for various values of $\bar{p}$ and sample sizes. An example would be—for our sample data—if we chose a fixed sample size of 25 for the future.

$$\bar{p} = .033 = 3.3\%$$

$$UCL_p = 14.0\%$$

Notice that the values given are percentages, to convert them to proportions divide by 100.

EXERCISE

7. Find the upper control limit using Table VI if

$$\bar{p} = 8.7\%$$
$$n = 50$$

INFORMATION

8. These values can be computed from σ_p (see frame 5) using the equations

$$UCL_p = \bar{p} + 3\sqrt{\frac{\bar{p}\,(1 - \bar{p})}{n}}$$

$$LCL_p = \bar{p} - 3\sqrt{\frac{\bar{p}\,(1 - \bar{p})}{n}}$$

Notice that if the sample size changes the control limits do too.

EXERCISE

8. Compute the upper and lower limits if

$$\bar{p} = 0.8\%$$
$$n = 75$$

INFORMATION

9. Should you choose to plot the **number** of defectives directly on the chart instead of the proportion defective, you can do so by computing the modified control limits for the value $n\bar{p}$ (sample size x the average proportion defectives).

$$UCL_{np} = n\bar{p} + 3\sqrt{n\bar{p}\,(1 - \bar{p})}$$

$$LCL_{np} = n\bar{p} - 3\sqrt{n\bar{p}\,(1 - \bar{p})}$$

For our example with n = 25:

$$n\bar{p} = 25(.033) = .825$$

$$UCL_{np} = 25(.033) + 3\sqrt{[25(.033)](1 - .033)}$$
$$= .825 + 2.680$$
$$= 3.5$$

$$LCL_{np} = 25(.033) - 3\sqrt{[25(.033)](1 - .033)}$$
$$= 0$$

Obviously, this will yield exactly the same results as the equivalent p chart above; however, you needn't compute the values of p with this chart—which could be a big plus in some applications. Table VII gives upper control limits for np charts for selected sample sizes and $\bar{p}$ values.

EXERCISE

9. Interpretation of p chart patterns is much different than interpretation of np charts.

____

True or False

INFORMATION

10. The interpretation of patterns inside the control limits for p charts, and np charts, is similar to the interpretation of patterns on $\overline{X}$ - R charts.

    You can say with very high confidence that the process is out of control for the proportion defective if any points fall beyond the control limits. Also, for $\overline{p}$ values of .10 or smaller, if five (5) consecutive points fall above the average.

    NOTE: **Do Not** calculate $\overline{p}$ (or process average proportions defective) by averaging the various p's; always calculate $\overline{p}$ as:

$$\frac{\text{TOTAL DEFECTIVES FOUND}}{\text{TOTAL NUMBER INSPECTED}}$$

11. You can, if you choose, plot the percent defective instead of the proportion defective (interpretation of the two is the same). Computing the average percent defective is done according to the following formula:

$$p' = \frac{\text{TOTAL NUMBER DEFECTIVE}}{\text{TOTAL NUMBER INSPECTED}} \times 100$$

    where p′ = Percent Defective.

    The control limits of a percent defective control chart are computed as follows:

$$UCLp' = p' + 3\sqrt{\frac{\overline{p}'(100 - \overline{p}')}{n}}$$

$$LCLp' = p' - 3\sqrt{\frac{\overline{p}'(100 - \overline{p}')}{n}}$$

    Table VI gives upper control limits for percent defective control charts with selected sample sizes.

12. In every chart discussed the lower control limit is set at zero if it is zero or negative. If the upper control limit is greater than 1 or 100% it is set equal to 1 or 100%.

13. At times, the appropriate measure of quality is the number of **defects per unit** (designated c) rather than the number **defective** in a sample. Such might be the case if the product is so complex that any unit might be expected to have some defects, or a very high proportion of the units. In such cases, the process quality can best be controled with the c Chart.

14. The c Chart is set up by a different formula than the other attribute control charts, but it is interpreted in the same way. Again, your first step is to determine the process average-in this case $\overline{c}$, the average number of defects per unit. This is computed as:

$$\overline{c} = \frac{\text{TOTAL NUMBER OF DEFECTS}}{\text{TOTAL PIECES INSPECTED}}$$

EXERCISES

10. Compute the average fraction defective for the data below:

	No. Insp.	No. Defective	p
	500	27	.054
	50	12	.240
	800	12	.015
	100	14	.140
	150	15	.100
TOTAL	1600	80	

11. What is the upper control limit if

    $\overline{p}' = 6.1\%$
    $n = 50$

13. A chart for defects per unit is called a

    ____

14. On c Charts, the center line is called

    ____

INFORMATION

15. The control limit lines for a c Chart are computed as follows:

$$UCL_c = \bar{c} + 3\sqrt{\bar{c}}$$

$$LCL_c = \bar{c} - 3\sqrt{\bar{c}}$$

16. As with most other attribute charts, the lower control limit is set at zero if it becomes negative.

A few applications for c Charts include:

— Errors per shipment of mail.
— Flaws per bolt of cloth.
— Defects per assembly.
— Paint defects per unit.

The data should indicate that the process is in statistical control before conclusions are drawn about process capability.

17. A variation of the c Chart is the u chart, which is simply a chart of the average number of defects per unit. While the normal sample for a c Chart is one unit, the u Chart is useful if the number of defects per unit is very small, or if some other reasons compel you to draw samples larger or smaller than one unit.

18. Interpretation of patterns on u Charts is identical to interpretation of other attribute control charts (see Frame 10). The center line for a u chart is called $\bar{u}$ and is computed:

$$\bar{u} = \frac{\text{NUMBER OF DEFECTS OBSERVED}}{\text{NUMBER OF ITEMS INSPECTED}}$$

The control limits for the u Chart are computed by a formula similar to that of the c Chart, namely:

$$UCL_u = \bar{u} + 3\sqrt{\frac{\bar{u}}{n}}$$

$$LCL_u = \bar{u} - 3\sqrt{\frac{\bar{u}}{n}}$$

19. AN IMPORTANT NOTE

The values of c and u are called "Poisson" variables; that is, they follow the poisson probability distribution. This is a probability distribution that is highly dependent on the size of the sample or inspection unit. You should take pains to keep the sample size and inspection unit constant for plottings on the c and u Charts.

20. It is important to take note that there are advance preparations that should be considered. These are the administrative and statistical aspects of quality control work. You should answer these questions before installing **any** control charts.

— Is the inspection unit clearly defined?
— Are the characteristics to be inspected measurable, clearly described, and documented?

EXERCISE

16. The c Chart lower control limit can be a negative number.

____

True or False

17. A u Chart is a control chart for:

____

INFORMATION

— Are the inspectors properly trained and informed?
— Do the inspectors have the proper data sheets to record their findings?
  - Does the data sheet adequately identify the product? The process? The inspection layout?
— Does the chart contain the essential information from the data sheet?
— Is the gaging adequate?
— Is provision made for investigation and corrective action when the chart indicates it is necessary?
— Is provision made for routine evaluation of control charts by trained personnel?
— Is provision made for periodic re-evaluation of control limits?

In short, is the statistical quality control program backed up by an effective total quality control program?

Attributes Control Charts
ANSWER KEY

FRAME	ANSWER
1	Attribute Characteristics
2	False
3	Proportion
4	Average Proportion Defective
5	Standard Deviation
6	True
7	UCL = 20.7%
8	LCL = 0 (see frame 5); UCL = 3.9%
9	False
10	$\bar{p}$ = 80/1600 = .05
11	16.3%
13	c Chart
14	c Bar
16	False, set it to zero if this occurs.
17	Average number of defects per unit.

APPENDIX

APPENDIX

APPENDIX

TABLE	SUBJECT
I	Runs
II	Control Chart Factors
III	Out of Control Criteria for Runs
IV	Process Capability Ratio Guide Lines
V	Cumulative Normal Distribution
VI	p Chart Upper Control Limits
VII	np Chart Upper Control Limits
VIII	Normal Areas
IX	Control Limit Formulas
X	Runs versus the Median

TABLE I.

RUNS ABOVE OR BELOW AVERAGE	PROBABILITY
1	.5
2	.25
3	.125
4	.0625
5	.03125
6	.0156
7	.0078
8	.0039
9	.00195
10	.00098

CHART	OUT OF CONTROL CRITERIA
$\overline{X}$, $\tilde{X}$, or R ($n \geq 3$)	1 point beyond 3 sigma line 2 of 3 points beyond 2 sigma line 4 of 5 points beyond 1 sigma line 7 in a row on same side of average
	13 in a row between −1 sigma and +1 sigma (stratification)
	5 in a row beyond −1 sigma and +1 sigma (mix)
p or np chart ($\overline{p} \leq .10$)	1 point beyond control limit
	5 in a row above average
Run chart*	

POINTS PLOTTED	MAX. CONSECUTIVE POINTS ON SAME SIDE OF $\tilde{X}$	MAX. CONSECUTIVE INCREASES OR DECREASES	MINIMUM NUMBER OF RUNS ABOVE AND BELOW $\tilde{X}$
10	—	6	—
20	8	7	4
30	9	7	8
40	10	7	12
50	11	7	16

*Freda S. Swwed and C. Eisenhart, "Tables for Testing Randomness of Groupings in a Sequence of Alternatives," *Annals of Mathematical Statistics*, Vol. XIV (1943), pp. 66-87.

TABLE II. Factors for Control Limits

NUMBER OF OBSERVATIONS IN SAMPLE, n	CHART FOR AVERAGES, FACTORS FOR CONTROL LIMITS A_2	CHART FOR RANGES			MEDIAN CHART
		d_2	D_3	D_4	$\tilde{A}_2$
2	1.880	1.128	0	3.267	—
3	1.023	1.693	0	2.575	1.187
4	0.729	2.059	0	2.282	—
5	0.577	2.326	0	2.115	0.691
6	0.483	2.534	0	2.004	—
7	0.419	2.704	0.076	1.924	0.508
8	0.373	2.847	0.136	1.864	—
9	0.337	2.970	0.184	1.816	.412
10	0.308	3.078	0.223	1.777	—
11	0.285	3.173	0.256	1.744	Medians not recommended for $n > 10$
12	0.266	3.258	0.284	1.716	
13	0.249	3.336	0.308	1.692	
14	0.235	3.407	0.329	1.671	
15	0.223	3.472	0.348	1.652	
16	0.212	3.532	0.364	1.636	
17	0.203	3.588	0.379	1.621	
18	0.194	3.640	0.392	1.608	
19	0.187	3.689	0.404	1.596	
20	0.180	3.735	0.414	1.586	
21	0.173	3.778	0.425	1.575	
22	0.167	3.819	0.434	1.566	
23	0.162	3.858	0.443	1.557	
24	0.157	3.895	0.452	1.548	
25	0.153	3.931	0.459	1.541	

TABLE III. Out-Of-Control Criteria

Consider the process out of control IF:

- 7 or more consecutive values exceed average
- 2 of 3 consecutive values exceed $\pm 2\sigma$
- 4 of 5 consecutive values exceed $\pm 1\sigma$
- Any value exceeds the 3σ control limit

TABLE IV. Capability Ratios

$$\text{Capability Ratio} = \frac{\text{TOLERANCE}}{\sigma} = \frac{\text{TOLERANCE}}{\overline{R}/d_2}$$

RATIO	SIGNIFICANCE
Less than 8.0	Process not capable of holding tolerance.
8.0 to 10	Capable process, requires close statistical control.
Over 10 to 20	Very capable process. Monitor with control charts or run charts.
20 or Greater	Extremely capable process. Can probably control with occasional audits, run charts.

TABLE V. Cumulative Normal Distribution — Values of p

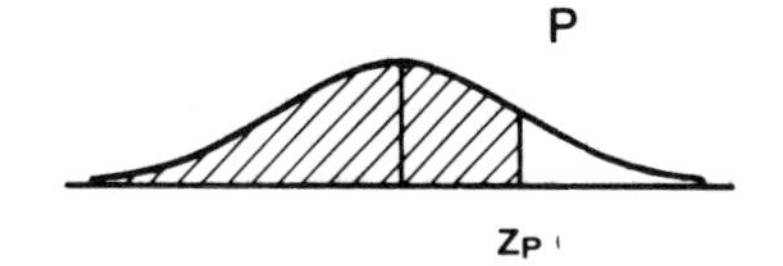

Values of P corresponding to z_P for the normal curve.

z is the standard normal variable. The value of P for $-z_P$ equals one minus the value of P for $+z_P$, e.g., the P for −1.62 equals 1 − .9474 = .0526.

z_P	.00	.01	.02	.03	.04	.05	.06	.07	.08	.09
.0	.5000	.5040	.5080	.5120	.5160	.5199	.5239	.5279	.5319	.5359
.1	.5398	.5438	.5478	.5517	.5557	.5596	.5636	.5675	.5714	.5753
.2	.5793	.5832	.5871	.5910	.5948	.5987	.6026	.6064	.6103	.6141
.3	.6179	.6217	.6255	.6293	.6331	.6368	.6406	.6443	.6480	.6517
.4	.6554	.6591	.6628	.6664	.6700	.6736	.6772	.6808	.6844	.6879
.5	.6915	.6950	.6985	.7019	.7054	.7088	.7123	.7157	.7190	.7224
.6	.7257	.7291	.7324	.7357	.7389	.7422	.7454	.7486	.7517	.7549
.7	.7580	.7611	.7642	.7673	.7704	.7734	.7764	.7794	.7823	.7852
.8	.7881	.7910	.7939	.7967	.7995	.8023	.8051	.8078	.8106	.8133
.9	.8159	.8186	.8212	.8238	.8264	.8289	.8315	.8340	.8365	.8389
1.0	.8413	.8438	.8461	.8485	.8508	.8531	.8554	.8577	.8599	.8621
1.1	.8643	.8665	.8686	.8708	.8729	.8749	.8770	.8790	.8810	.8830
1.2	.8849	.8869	.8888	.8907	.8925	.8944	.8962	.8980	.8997	.9015
1.3	.9032	.9049	.9066	.9082	.9099	.9115	.9131	.9147	.9162	.9177
1.4	.9192	.9207	.9222	.9236	.9251	.9265	.9279	.9292	.9306	.9319
1.5	.9332	.9345	.9357	.9370	.9382	.9394	.9406	.9418	.9429	.9441
1.6	.9452	.9463	.9474	.9484	.9495	.9505	.9515	.9525	.9535	.9545
1.7	.9554	.9564	.9573	.9582	.9591	.9599	.9608	.9616	.9625	.9633
1.8	.9641	.9649	.9656	.9664	.9671	.9678	.9686	.9693	.9699	.9706
1.9	.9713	.9719	.9726	.9732	.9738	.9744	.9750	.9756	.9761	.9767
2.0	.9772	.9778	.9783	.9788	.9793	.9798	.9803	.9808	.9812	.9817
2.1	.9821	.9826	.9830	.9834	.9838	.9842	.9846	.9850	.9854	.9857
2.2	.9861	.9864	.9868	.9871	.9875	.9878	.9881	.9884	.9887	.9890
2.3	.9893	.9896	.9898	.9901	.9904	.9906	.9909	.9911	.9913	.9916
2.4	.9918	.9920	.9922	.9925	.9927	.9929	.9931	.9932	.9934	.9936
2.5	.9938	.9940	.9941	.9943	.9945	.9946	.9948	.9949	.9951	.9952
2.6	.9953	.9955	.9956	.9957	.9959	.9960	.9961	.9962	.9963	.9964
2.7	.9965	.9966	.9967	.9968	.9969	.9970	.9971	.9972	.9973	.9974
2.8	.9974	.9975	.9976	.9977	.9977	.9978	.9979	.9979	.9980	.9981
2.9	.9981	.9982	.9982	.9983	.9984	.9984	.9985	.9985	.9986	.9986
3.0	.9987	.9987	.9987	.9988	.9988	.9989	.9989	.9989	.9990	.9990
3.1	.9990	.9991	.9991	.9991	.9992	.9992	.9992	.9992	.9993	.9993
3.2	.9993	.9993	.9994	.9994	.9994	.9994	.9994	.9995	.9995	.9995
3.3	.9995	.9995	.9995	.9996	.9996	.9996	.9996	.9996	.9996	.9997
3.4	.9997	.9997	.9997	.9997	.9997	.9997	.9997	.9997	.9997	.9998

TABLE VI. p Chart — Upper Control Limits

AVG % DEF	n=10	n=20	n=25	n=50	n=100
0.1	3.1	2.2	2.0	1.4	1.0
0.2	4.4	3.2	2.9	2.1	1.5
0.3	5.5	4.0	3.6	2.6	1.9
0.4	6.4	4.6	4.2	3.1	2.3
0.5	7.2	5.2	4.7	3.5	2.6
0.6	7.9	5.8	5.2	3.9	2.9
0.7	8.6	6.3	5.7	4.2	3.2
0.8	9.3	6.8	6.1	4.6	3.5
0.9	9.9	7.2	6.6	4.9	3.7
1.0	10.4	7.7	7.0	5.2	4.0
1.1	11.0	8.1	7.4	5.5	4.2
1.2	11.5	8.5	7.7	5.8	4.5
1.3	12.0	8.9	8.1	6.1	4.7
1.4	12.5	9.3	8.4	6.4	4.9
1.5	13.0	9.7	8.8	6.7	5.1
1.6	13.5	10.0	9.1	6.9	5.4
1.7	14.0	10.4	9.5	7.2	5.6
1.8	14.4	10.7	9.8	7.4	5.8
1.9	14.9	11.1	10.1	7.7	6.0
2.0	15.3	11.4	10.4	7.9	6.2
2.1	15.7	11.7	10.7	8.2	6.4
2.2	16.1	12.0	11.0	8.4	6.6
2.3	16.5	12.4	11.3	8.7	6.8
2.4	16.9	12.7	11.6	8.9	7.0
2.5	17.3	13.0	11.9	9.1	7.2
2.6	17.7	13.3	12.1	9.4	7.4
2.7	18.1	13.6	12.4	9.6	7.6
2.8	18.5	13.9	12.7	9.8	7.7
2.9	18.8	14.2	13.0	10.0	7.9
3.0	19.2	14.4	13.2	10.2	8.1
3.1	19.5	14.7	13.5	10.5	8.3
3.2	19.9	15.0	13.8	10.7	8.5
3.3	20.2	15.3	14.0	10.9	8.7
3.4	20.6	15.6	14.3	11.1	8.8
3.5	20.9	15.8	14.5	11.3	9.0
3.6	21.3	16.1	14.8	11.5	9.2
3.7	21.6	16.4	15.0	11.7	9.4
3.8	21.9	16.6	15.3	11.9	9.5
3.9	22.3	16.9	15.5	12.1	9.7
4.0	22.6	17.1	15.8	12.3	9.9
4.1	22.9	17.4	16.0	12.5	10.0
4.2	23.2	17.7	16.2	12.7	10.2
4.3	23.5	17.9	16.5	12.9	10.4
4.4	23.9	18.2	16.7	13.1	10.6
4.5	24.2	18.4	16.9	13.3	10.7
4.6	24.5	18.7	17.2	13.5	10.9
4.7	24.8	18.9	17.4	13.7	11.0
4.8	25.1	19.1	17.6	13.9	11.2
4.9	25.4	19.4	17.9	14.1	11.4

AVG % DEF	n=10	n=20	n=25	n=50	n=100
5.0	25.7	19.6	18.1	14.2	11.5
5.1	26.0	19.9	18.3	14.4	11.7
5.2	26.3	20.1	18.5	14.6	11.9
5.3	26.6	20.3	18.7	14.8	12.0
5.4	26.8	20.6	19.0	15.0	12.2
5.5	27.1	20.8	19.2	15.2	12.3
5.6	27.4	21.0	19.4	15.4	12.5
5.7	27.7	21.3	19.6	15.5	12.7
5.8	28.0	21.5	19.8	15.7	12.8
5.9	28.3	21.7	20.0	15.9	13.0
6.0	28.5	21.9	20.2	16.1	13.1
6.1	28.8	22.2	20.5	16.3	13.3
6.2	29.1	22.4	20.7	16.4	13.4
6.3	29.3	22.6	20.9	16.6	13.6
6.4	29.6	22.8	21.1	16.8	13.7
6.5	29.9	23.0	21.3	17.0	13.9
6.6	30.2	23.3	21.5	17.1	14.0
6.7	30.4	23.5	21.7	17.3	14.2
6.8	30.7	23.7	21.9	17.5	14.4
6.9	30.9	23.9	22.1	17.7	14.5
7.0	31.2	24.1	22.3	17.8	14.7
7.1	31.5	24.3	22.5	18.0	14.8
7.2	31.7	24.5	22.7	18.2	15.0
7.3	32.0	24.8	22.9	18.3	15.1
7.4	32.2	25.0	23.1	18.5	15.3
7.5	32.5	25.2	23.3	18.7	15.4
7.6	32.7	25.4	23.5	18.8	15.5
7.7	33.0	25.6	23.7	19.0	15.7
7.8	33.2	25.8	23.9	19.2	15.8
7.9	33.5	26.0	24.1	19.3	16.0
8.0	33.7	26.2	24.3	19.5	16.1
8.1	34.0	26.4	24.5	19.7	16.3
8.2	34.2	26.6	24.7	19.8	16.4
8.3	34.5	26.8	24.9	20.0	16.6
8.4	34.7	27.0	25.0	20.2	16.7
8.5	35.0	27.2	25.2	20.3	16.9
8.6	35.2	27.4	25.4	20.5	17.0
8.7	35.4	27.6	25.6	20.7	17.2
8.8	35.7	27.8	25.8	20.8	17.3
8.9	35.9	28.0	26.0	21.0	17.4
9.0	36.1	28.2	26.2	21.1	17.6
9.1	36.4	28.4	26.4	21.3	17.7
9.2	36.6	28.6	26.5	21.5	17.9
9.3	36.9	28.8	26.7	21.6	18.0
9.4	37.1	29.0	26.9	21.8	18.2
9.5	37.3	29.2	27.1	21.9	18.3
9.6	37.5	29.4	27.3	22.1	18.4
9.7	37.8	29.6	27.5	22.3	18.6
9.8	38.0	29.7	27.6	22.4	18.7

AVG % DEF	n=10	n=20	n=25	n=50	n=100
9.9	38.2	29.9	27.8	22.6	18.9
10.0	38.5	30.1	28.0	22.7	19.0
10.1	38.7	30.3	28.2	22.9	19.1
10.2	38.9	30.5	28.4	23.0	19.3
10.3	39.1	30.7	28.5	23.2	19.4
10.4	39.4	30.9	28.7	23.4	19.6
10.5	39.6	31.1	28.9	23.5	19.7
10.6	39.8	31.3	29.1	23.7	19.8
10.7	40.0	31.4	29.2	23.8	20.0
10.8	40.2	31.6	29.4	24.0	20.1
10.9	40.5	31.8	29.6	24.1	20.2
11.0	40.7	32.0	29.8	24.3	20.4
11.1	40.9	32.2	29.9	24.4	20.5
11.2	41.1	32.4	30.1	24.6	20.7
11.3	41.3	32.5	30.3	24.7	20.8
11.4	41.6	32.7	30.5	24.9	20.9
11.5	41.8	32.9	30.6	25.0	21.1
11.6	42.0	33.1	30.8	25.2	21.2
11.7	42.2	33.3	31.0	25.3	21.3
11.8	42.4	33.4	31.2	25.5	21.5
11.9	42.6	33.6	31.3	25.6	21.6
12.0	42.8	33.8	31.5	25.8	21.7
12.1	43.0	34.0	31.7	25.9	21.9
12.2	43.2	34.2	31.8	26.1	22.0
12.3	43.5	34.3	32.0	26.2	22.2
12.4	43.7	34.5	32.2	26.4	22.3
12.5	43.9	34.7	32.3	26.5	22.4
12.6	44.1	34.9	32.5	26.7	22.6
12.7	44.3	35.0	32.7	26.8	22.7
12.8	44.5	35.2	32.8	27.0	22.8
12.9	44.7	35.4	33.0	27.1	23.0
13.0	44.9	35.6	33.2	27.3	23.1
13.1	45.1	35.7	33.3	27.4	23.2
13.2	45.3	35.9	33.5	27.6	23.4
13.3	45.5	36.1	33.7	27.7	23.5
13.4	45.7	36.3	33.8	27.9	23.6
13.5	45.9	36.4	34.0	28.0	23.8
13.6	46.1	36.6	34.2	28.1	23.9
13.7	46.3	36.8	34.3	28.3	24.0
13.8	46.5	36.9	34.5	28.4	24.1
13.9	46.7	37.1	34.7	28.6	24.3
14.0	46.9	37.3	34.8	28.7	24.4
14.1	47.1	37.4	35.0	28.9	24.5
14.2	47.3	37.6	35.1	29.0	24.7
14.3	47.5	37.8	35.3	29.2	24.8
14.4	47.7	38.0	35.5	29.3	24.9
14.5	47.9	38.1	35.6	29.4	25.1
14.6	48.1	38.3	35.8	29.6	25.2
14.7	48.3	38.5	35.9	29.7	25.3

TABLE VI. p Chart — Upper Control Limits, cont'd

AVG % DEF	n=10	n=20	n=25	n=50	n=100
14.8	48.5	38.6	36.1	29.9	25.5
14.9	48.7	38.8	36.3	30.0	25.6
15.0	48.9	39.0	36.4	30.1	25.7
15.1	49.1	39.1	36.6	30.3	25.8
15.2	49.3	39.3	36.7	30.4	26.0
15.3	49.5	39.4	36.9	30.6	26.1
15.4	49.6	39.6	37.1	30.7	26.2
15.5	49.8	39.8	37.2	30.9	26.4
15.6	50.0	39.9	37.4	31.0	26.5
15.7	50.2	40.1	37.5	31.1	26.6
15.8	50.4	40.3	37.7	31.3	26.7
15.9	50.6	40.4	37.8	31.4	26.9
16.0	50.8	40.6	38.0	31.6	27.0
16.1	51.0	40.8	38.2	31.7	27.1
16.2	51.2	40.9	38.3	31.8	27.3
16.3	51.3	41.1	38.5	32.0	27.4
16.4	51.5	41.2	38.6	32.1	27.5
16.5	51.7	41.4	38.8	32.2	27.6
16.6	51.9	41.6	38.9	32.4	27.8
16.7	52.1	41.7	39.1	32.5	27.9
16.8	52.3	41.9	39.2	32.7	28.0
16.9	52.5	42.0	39.4	32.8	28.1
17.0	52.6	42.2	39.5	32.9	28.3
17.1	52.8	42.4	39.7	33.1	28.4
17.2	53.0	42.5	39.8	33.2	28.5
17.3	53.2	42.7	40.0	33.3	28.6
17.4	53.4	42.8	40.1	33.5	28.8
17.5	53.5	43.0	40.3	33.6	28.9
17.6	53.7	43.1	40.4	33.8	29.0
17.7	53.9	43.3	40.6	33.9	29.2
17.8	54.1	43.5	40.8	34.0	29.3
17.9	54.3	43.6	40.9	34.2	29.4
18.0	54.4	43.8	41.1	34.3	29.5
18.1	54.6	43.9	41.2	34.4	29.7

AVG % DEF	n=10	n=20	n=25	n=50	n=100
18.2	54.8	44.1	41.4	34.6	29.8
18.3	55.0	44.2	41.5	34.7	29.9
18.4	55.2	44.4	41.6	34.8	30.0
18.5	55.3	44.5	41.8	35.0	30.1
18.6	55.5	44.7	41.9	35.1	30.3
18.7	55.7	44.9	42.1	35.2	30.4
18.8	55.9	45.0	42.2	35.4	30.5
18.9	56.0	45.2	42.4	35.5	30.6
19.0	56.2	45.3	42.5	35.6	30.8
19.1	56.4	45.5	42.7	35.8	30.9
19.2	56.6	45.6	42.8	35.9	31.0
19.3	56.7	45.8	43.0	36.0	31.1
19.4	56.9	45.9	43.1	36.2	31.3
19.5	57.1	46.1	43.3	36.3	31.4
19.6	57.3	46.2	43.4	36.4	31.5
19.7	57.4	46.4	43.6	36.6	31.6
19.8	57.6	46.5	43.7	36.7	31.8
19.9	57.8	46.7	43.9	36.8	31.9
20.0	57.9	46.8	44.0	37.0	32.0
20.1	58.1	47.0	44.1	37.1	32.1
20.2	58.3	47.1	44.3	37.2	32.2
20.3	58.5	47.3	44.4	37.4	32.4
20.4	58.6	47.4	44.6	37.5	32.5
20.5	58.8	47.6	44.7	37.6	32.6
20.6	59.0	47.7	44.9	37.8	32.7
20.7	59.1	47.9	45.0	37.9	32.9
20.8	59.3	48.0	45.2	38.0	33.0
20.9	59.5	48.2	45.3	38.2	33.1
21.0	59.6	48.3	45.4	38.3	33.2
21.1	59.8	48.5	45.6	38.4	33.3
21.2	60.0	48.6	45.7	38.5	33.5
21.3	60.1	48.8	45.9	38.7	33.6
21.4	60.3	48.9	46.0	38.8	33.7
21.5	60.5	49.1	46.1	38.9	33.8
21.6	60.6	49.2	46.3	39.1	33.9

AVG % DEF	n=10	n=20	n=25	n=50	n=100
21.7	60.8	49.4	46.4	39.2	34.1
21.8	61.0	49.5	46.6	39.3	34.2
21.9	61.1	49.6	46.7	39.4	34.3
22.0	61.3	49.8	46.9	39.6	34.4
22.1	61.5	49.9	47.0	39.7	34.5
22.2	61.6	50.1	47.1	39.8	34.7
22.3	61.8	50.2	47.3	40.0	34.8
22.4	62.0	50.4	47.4	40.1	34.9
22.5	62.1	50.5	47.6	40.2	35.0
22.6	62.3	50.7	47.7	40.3	35.1
22.7	62.4	50.8	47.8	40.5	35.3
22.8	62.6	50.9	48.0	40.6	35.4
22.9	62.8	51.1	48.1	40.7	35.5
23.0	62.9	51.2	48.2	40.9	35.6
23.1	63.1	51.4	48.4	41.0	35.7
23.2	63.2	51.5	48.5	41.1	35.9
23.3	63.4	51.7	48.7	41.2	36.0
23.4	63.6	51.8	48.8	41.4	36.1
23.5	63.7	51.9	48.9	41.5	36.2
23.6	63.9	52.1	49.1	41.6	36.3
23.7	64.0	52.2	49.2	41.7	36.5
23.8	64.2	52.4	49.4	41.9	36.6
23.9	64.4	52.5	49.5	42.0	36.7
24.0	64.5	52.6	49.6	42.1	36.8
24.1	64.7	52.8	49.8	42.2	36.9
24.2	64.8	52.9	49.9	42.4	37.0
24.3	65.0	53.1	50.0	42.5	37.2
24.4	65.1	53.2	50.2	42.6	37.3
24.5	65.3	53.4	50.3	42.7	37.4
24.6	65.5	53.5	50.4	42.9	37.5
24.7	65.6	53.6	50.6	43.0	37.6
24.8	65.8	53.8	50.7	43.1	37.8
24.9	65.9	53.9	50.8	43.2	37.9
25.0	66.1	54.0	51.0	43.4	38.0

TABLE VII. np Chart — Upper Control Limits

AVG % DEF	n=10	n=20	n=25	n=50	n=100
0.1	0.3	0.4	0.5	0.7	1.0
0.2	0.4	0.6	0.7	1.0	1.5
0.3	0.5	0.8	0.9	1.3	1.9
0.4	0.6	0.9	1.0	1.5	2.3
0.5	0.7	1.0	1.2	1.7	2.6
0.6	0.8	1.2	1.3	1.9	2.9
0.7	0.9	1.3	1.4	2.1	3.2
0.8	0.9	1.4	1.5	2.3	3.5
0.9	1.0	1.4	1.6	2.5	3.7
1.0	1.0	1.5	1.7	2.6	4.0
1.1	1.1	1.6	1.8	2.8	4.2
1.2	1.2	1.7	1.9	2.9	4.5
1.3	1.2	1.8	2.0	3.1	4.7
1.4	1.3	1.9	2.1	3.2	4.9
1.5	1.3	1.9	2.2	3.3	5.1
1.6	1.4	2.0	2.3	3.5	5.4
1.7	1.4	2.1	2.4	3.6	5.6
1.8	1.4	2.1	2.4	3.7	5.8
1.9	1.5	2.2	2.5	3.8	6.0
2.0	1.5	2.3	2.6	4.0	6.2
2.1	1.6	2.3	2.7	4.1	6.4
2.2	1.6	2.4	2.8	4.2	6.6
2.3	1.7	2.5	2.8	4.3	6.8
2.4	1.7	2.5	2.9	4.4	7.0
2.5	1.7	2.6	3.0	4.6	7.2
2.6	1.8	2.7	3.0	4.7	7.4
2.7	1.8	2.7	3.1	4.8	7.6
2.8	1.8	2.8	3.2	4.9	7.7
2.9	1.9	2.8	3.2	5.0	7.9
3.0	1.9	2.9	3.3	5.1	8.1
3.1	2.0	2.9	3.4	5.2	8.3
3.2	2.0	3.0	3.4	5.3	8.5
3.3	2.0	3.1	3.5	5.4	8.7
3.4	2.1	3.1	3.6	5.5	8.8
3.5	2.1	3.2	3.6	5.6	9.0
3.6	2.1	3.2	3.7	5.8	9.2
3.7	2.2	3.3	3.8	5.9	9.4
3.8	2.2	3.3	3.8	6.0	9.5
3.9	2.2	3.4	3.9	6.1	9.7
4.0	2.3	3.4	3.9	6.2	9.9
4.1	2.3	3.5	4.0	6.3	10.0
4.2	2.3	3.5	4.1	6.4	10.2
4.3	2.4	3.6	4.1	6.5	10.4
4.4	2.4	3.6	4.2	6.6	10.6
4.5	2.4	3.7	4.2	6.6	10.7
4.6	2.4	3.7	4.3	6.7	10.9
4.7	2.5	3.8	4.3	6.8	11.0
4.8	2.5	3.8	4.4	6.9	11.2
4.9	2.5	3.9	4.5	7.0	11.4

AVG % DEF	n=10	n=20	n=25	n=50	n=100
5.0	2.6	3.9	4.5	7.1	11.5
5.1	2.6	4.0	4.6	7.2	11.7
5.2	2.6	4.0	4.6	7.3	11.9
5.3	2.7	4.1	4.7	7.4	12.0
5.4	2.7	4.1	4.7	7.5	12.2
5.5	2.7	4.2	4.8	7.6	12.3
5.6	2.7	4.2	4.8	7.7	12.5
5.7	2.8	4.3	4.9	7.8	12.7
5.8	2.8	4.3	5.0	7.9	12.8
5.9	2.8	4.3	5.0	7.9	13.0
6.0	2.9	4.4	5.1	8.0	13.1
6.1	2.9	4.4	5.1	8.1	13.3
6.2	2.9	4.5	5.2	8.2	13.4
6.3	2.9	4.5	5.2	8.3	13.6
6.4	3.0	4.6	5.3	8.4	13.7
6.5	3.0	4.6	5.3	8.5	13.9
6.6	3.0	4.7	5.4	8.6	14.0
6.7	3.0	4.7	5.4	8.7	14.2
6.8	3.1	4.7	5.5	8.7	14.4
6.9	3.1	4.8	5.5	8.8	14.5
7.0	3.1	4.8	5.6	8.9	14.7
7.1	3.1	4.9	5.6	9.0	14.8
7.2	3.2	4.9	5.7	9.1	15.0
7.3	3.2	5.0	5.7	9.2	15.1
7.4	3.2	5.0	5.8	9.3	15.3
7.5	3.2	5.0	5.8	9.3	15.4
7.6	3.3	5.1	5.9	9.4	15.5
7.7	3.3	5.1	5.9	9.5	15.7
7.8	3.3	5.2	6.0	9.6	15.8
7.9	3.3	5.2	6.0	9.7	16.0
8.0	3.4	5.2	6.1	9.8	16.1
8.1	3.4	5.3	6.1	9.8	16.3
8.2	3.4	5.3	6.2	9.9	16.4
8.3	3.4	5.4	6.2	10.0	16.6
8.4	3.5	5.4	6.3	10.1	16.7
8.5	3.5	5.4	6.3	10.2	16.9
8.6	3.5	5.5	6.4	10.2	17.0
8.7	3.5	5.5	6.4	10.3	17.2
8.8	3.6	5.6	6.4	10.4	17.3
8.9	3.6	5.6	6.5	10.5	17.4
9.0	3.6	5.6	6.5	10.6	17.6
9.1	3.6	5.7	6.6	10.7	17.7
9.2	3.7	5.7	6.6	10.7	17.9
9.3	3.7	5.8	6.7	10.8	18.0
9.4	3.7	5.8	6.7	10.9	18.2
9.5	3.7	5.8	6.8	11.0	18.3
9.6	3.8	5.9	6.8	11.0	18.4
9.7	3.8	5.9	6.9	11.1	18.6
9.8	3.8	5.9	6.9	11.2	18.7

AVG % DEF	n=10	n=20	n=25	n=50	n=100
9.9	3.8	6.0	7.0	11.3	18.9
10.0	3.8	6.0	7.0	11.4	19.0
10.1	3.9	6.1	7.0	11.4	19.1
10.2	3.9	6.1	7.1	11.5	19.3
10.3	3.9	6.1	7.1	11.6	19.4
10.4	3.9	6.2	7.2	11.7	19.6
10.5	4.0	6.2	7.2	11.8	19.7
10.6	4.0	6.3	7.3	11.8	19.8
10.7	4.0	6.3	7.3	11.9	20.0
10.8	4.0	6.3	7.4	12.0	20.1
10.9	4.0	6.4	7.4	12.1	20.2
11.0	4.1	6.4	7.4	12.1	20.4
11.1	4.1	6.4	7.5	12.2	20.5
11.2	4.1	6.5	7.5	12.3	20.7
11.3	4.1	6.5	7.6	12.4	20.8
11.4	4.2	6.5	7.6	12.4	20.9
11.5	4.2	6.6	7.7	12.5	21.1
11.6	4.2	6.6	7.7	12.6	21.2
11.7	4.2	6.7	7.7	12.7	21.3
11.8	4.2	6.7	7.8	12.7	21.5
11.9	4.3	6.7	7.8	12.8	21.6
12.0	4.3	6.8	7.9	12.9	21.7
12.1	4.3	6.8	7.9	13.0	21.9
12.2	4.3	6.8	8.0	13.0	22.0
12.3	4.3	6.9	8.0	13.1	22.2
12.4	4.4	6.9	8.0	13.2	22.3
12.5	4.4	6.9	8.1	13.3	22.4
12.6	4.4	7.0	8.1	13.3	22.6
12.7	4.4	7.0	8.2	13.4	22.7
12.8	4.4	7.0	8.2	13.5	22.8
12.9	4.5	7.1	8.3	13.6	23.0
13.0	4.5	7.1	8.3	13.6	23.1
13.1	4.5	7.1	8.3	13.7	23.2
13.2	4.5	7.2	8.4	13.8	23.4
13.3	4.6	7.3	8.4	13.9	23.5
13.4	4.6	7.3	8.5	13.9	23.6
13.5	4.6	7.3	8.5	14.0	23.8
13.6	4.6	7.3	8.5	14.1	23.9
13.7	4.6	7.4	8.6	14.1	24.0
13.8	4.7	7.4	8.6	14.2	24.1
13.9	4.7	7.4	8.7	14.3	24.3
14.0	4.7	7.5	8.7	14.4	24.4
14.1	4.7	7.5	8.7	14.4	24.5
14.2	4.7	7.5	8.8	14.5	24.7
14.3	4.8	7.6	8.8	14.6	24.8
14.4	4.8	7.6	8.9	14.6	24.9
14.5	4.8	7.6	8.9	14.7	25.1
14.6	4.8	7.7	8.9	14.8	25.2
14.7	4.8	7.7	9.0	14.9	25.3

TABLE VII. np Chart — Upper Control Limits, cont'd

AVG % DEF	n=10	n=20	n=25	n=50	n=100
14.8	4.8	7.7	9.0	14.9	25.5
14.9	4.9	7.8	9.1	15.0	25.6
15.0	4.9	7.8	9.1	15.1	25.7
15.1	4.9	7.8	9.1	15.1	25.8
15.2	4.9	7.9	9.2	15.2	26.0
15.3	4.9	7.9	9.2	15.3	26.1
15.4	5.0	7.9	9.3	15.4	26.2
15.5	5.0	8.0	9.3	15.4	26.4
15.6	5.0	8.0	9.3	15.5	26.5
15.7	5.0	8.0	9.4	15.6	26.6
15.8	5.0	8.1	9.4	15.6	26.7
15.9	5.1	8.1	9.5	15.7	26.9
16.0	5.1	8.1	9.5	15.8	27.0
16.1	5.1	8.2	9.5	15.8	27.1
16.2	5.1	8.2	9.6	15.9	27.3
16.3	5.1	8.2	9.6	16.0	27.4
16.4	5.2	8.2	9.7	16.1	27.5
16.5	5.2	8.3	9.7	16.1	27.6
16.6	5.2	8.3	9.7	16.2	27.8
16.7	5.2	8.3	9.8	16.3	27.9
16.8	5.2	8.4	9.8	16.3	28.0
16.9	5.2	8.4	9.8	16.4	28.1
17.0	5.3	8.4	9.9	16.5	28.3
17.1	5.3	8.5	9.9	16.5	28.4
17.2	5.3	8.5	10.0	16.6	28.5
17.3	5.3	8.5	10.0	16.7	28.6
17.4	5.3	8.6	10.0	16.7	28.8
17.5	5.4	8.6	10.1	16.8	28.9
17.6	5.4	8.6	10.1	16.9	29.0
17.7	5.4	8.7	10.2	16.9	29.2
17.8	5.4	8.7	10.2	17.0	29.3
17.9	5.4	8.7	10.2	17.1	29.4
18.0	5.4	8.8	10.3	17.1	29.5
18.1	5.5	8.8	10.3	17.2	29.7

AVG % DEF	n=10	n=20	n=25	n=50	n=100
18.2	5.5	8.8	10.3	17.3	29.8
18.3	5.5	8.8	10.4	17.4	29.9
18.4	5.5	8.9	10.4	17.4	30.0
18.5	5.5	8.9	10.4	17.5	30.1
18.6	5.6	8.9	10.5	17.6	30.3
18.7	5.6	9.0	10.5	17.6	30.4
18.8	5.6	9.0	10.6	17.7	30.5
18.9	5.6	9.0	10.6	17.8	30.6
19.0	5.6	9.1	10.6	17.8	30.8
19.1	5.6	9.1	10.7	17.9	30.9
19.2	5.7	9.1	10.7	18.0	31.0
19.3	5.7	9.2	10.7	18.0	31.1
19.4	5.7	9.2	10.8	18.1	31.3
19.5	5.7	9.2	10.8	18.2	31.4
19.6	5.7	9.2	10.9	18.2	31.5
19.7	5.7	9.3	10.9	18.3	31.6
19.8	5.8	9.3	10.9	18.4	31.8
19.9	5.8	9.3	11.0	18.4	31.9
20.0	5.8	9.4	11.0	18.5	32.0
20.1	5.8	9.4	11.0	18.6	32.1
20.2	5.8	9.4	11.1	18.6	32.2
20.3	5.8	9.5	11.1	18.7	32.4
20.4	5.9	9.5	11.1	18.7	32.5
20.5	5.9	9.5	11.2	18.8	32.6
20.6	5.9	9.5	11.2	18.9	32.7
20.7	5.9	9.6	11.3	18.9	32.9
20.8	5.9	9.6	11.3	19.0	33.0
20.9	5.9	9.6	11.3	19.1	33.1
21.0	6.0	9.7	11.4	19.1	33.2
21.1	6.0	9.7	11.4	19.2	33.3
21.2	6.0	9.7	11.4	19.3	33.5
21.3	6.0	9.8	11.5	19.3	33.6
21.4	6.0	9.8	11.5	19.4	33.7
21.5	6.0	9.8	11.5	19.5	33.8
21.6	6.1	9.8	11.6	19.5	33.9

AVG % DEF	n=10	n=20	n=25	n=50	n=100
21.7	6.1	9.9	11.6	19.6	34.1
21.8	6.1	9.9	11.6	19.7	34.2
21.9	6.1	9.9	11.7	19.7	34.3
22.0	6.1	10.0	11.7	19.8	34.4
22.1	6.1	10.0	11.7	19.9	34.5
22.2	6.2	10.0	11.8	19.9	34.7
22.3	6.2	10.0	11.8	20.0	34.8
22.4	6.2	10.1	11.9	20.0	34.9
22.5	6.2	10.1	11.9	20.1	35.0
22.6	6.2	10.1	11.9	20.2	35.1
22.7	6.2	10.2	12.0	20.2	35.3
22.8	6.3	10.2	12.0	20.3	35.4
22.9	6.3	10.2	12.0	20.4	35.5
23.0	6.3	10.2	12.1	20.4	35.6
23.1	6.3	10.3	12.1	20.5	35.7
23.2	6.3	10.3	12.1	20.6	35.9
23.3	6.3	10.3	12.2	20.6	36.0
23.4	6.4	10.4	12.2	20.7	36.1
23.5	6.4	10.4	12.2	20.7	36.2
23.6	6.4	10.4	12.3	20.8	36.3
23.7	6.4	10.4	12.3	20.9	36.5
23.8	6.4	10.4	12.3	20.9	36.6
23.9	6.4	10.5	12.4	21.0	36.7
24.0	6.5	10.5	12.4	21.1	36.8
24.1	6.5	10.6	12.4	21.1	36.9
24.2	6.5	10.6	12.5	21.2	37.0
24.3	6.5	10.6	12.5	21.2	37.2
24.4	6.5	10.6	12.5	21.3	37.3
24.5	6.5	10.7	12.6	21.4	37.4
24.6	6.5	10.7	12.6	21.4	37.5
24.7	6.6	10.7	12.6	21.5	37.6
24.8	6.6	10.8	12.7	21.6	37.8
24.9	6.6	10.8	12.7	21.6	37.9
25.0	6.6	10.8	12.7	21.7	38.0

TABLE VIII. Normal Distribution Areas

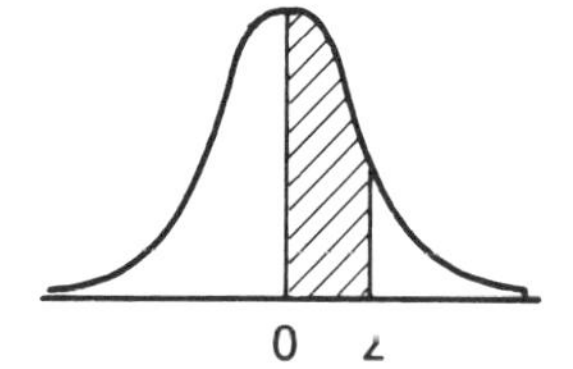

Each figure in the body of the table is preceded by a decimal point.

z	0.00	0.01	0.02	0.03	0.04	0.05	0.06	0.07	0.08	0.09
0.0	00000	00399	00798	01197	01595	01994	02392	02790	03188	03586
0.1	03983	04380	04776	05172	05567	05962	06356	06749	07142	07535
0.2	07926	08317	08706	09095	09483	09871	10257	10642	11026	11409
0.3	11791	12172	12552	12930	13307	13683	14058	14431	14803	15173
0.4	15554	15910	16276	16640	17003	17364	17724	18082	18439	18793
0.5	19146	19497	19847	20194	20540	20884	21226	21566	21904	22240
0.6	22575	22907	23237	23565	23891	24215	24537	24857	25175	25490
0.7	25804	26115	26424	26730	27035	27337	27637	27935	28230	28524
0.8	28814	29103	29389	29673	29955	30234	30511	30785	31057	31327
0.9	31594	31859	32121	32381	32639	32894	33147	33398	33646	33891
1.0	34134	34375	34614	34850	35083	35313	35543	35769	35993	36214
1.1	36433	36650	36864	37076	37286	37493	37698	37900	38100	38298
1.2	38493	38686	38877	39065	39251	39435	39617	39796	39973	40147
1.3	40320	40490	40658	40824	40988	41149	41308	41466	41621	41774
1.4	41924	42073	42220	42364	42507	42647	42786	42922	43056	43189
1.5	43319	43448	43574	43699	43822	43943	44062	44179	44295	44408
1.6	44520	44630	44738	44845	44950	45053	45154	45254	45352	45449
1.7	45543	45637	45728	45818	45907	45994	46080	46164	46246	46327
1.8	46407	46485	46562	46638	46712	46784	46856	46926	46995	47062
1.9	47128	47193	47257	47320	47381	47441	47500	47558	47615	47670
2.0	47725	47778	47831	47882	47932	47982	48030	48077	48124	48169
2.1	48214	48257	48300	48341	48382	48422	48461	48500	48537	48574
2.2	48610	48645	48679	48713	48745	48778	48809	48840	48870	48899
2.3	48928	48956	48983	49010	49036	49061	49086	49111	49134	49158
2.4	49180	49202	49224	49245	49266	49286	49305	49324	49343	49361
2.5	49379	49396	49413	49430	49446	49461	49477	49492	49506	49520
2.6	49534	49547	49560	49573	49585	49598	49609	49621	49632	49643
2.7	49653	49664	49674	49683	49693	49702	49711	49720	49728	49736
2.8	49744	49752	49760	49767	49774	49781	49788	49795	49801	49807
2.9	49813	49819	49825	49831	49836	49841	49846	49851	49856	49861
3.0	49865	49869	49874	49878	49882	49886	49889	49893	49896	49900
3.1	49903	49906	49910	49913	49915	49918	49921	49924	49926	49929
3.2	49931	49934	49936	49938	49940	49942	49944	49946	49948	49950
3.3	49952	49953	49955	49957	49958	49960	49961	49962	49964	49965

TABLE IX. Control Limit Formulas

CHART	UPPER CONTROL LIMIT	LOWER CONTROL LIMIT
$\overline{X}$	$\overline{\overline{X}} + A_2\overline{R}$	$\overline{\overline{X}} - A_2\overline{R}$
R	$D_4\overline{R}$	$D_3\overline{R}$
p (Proportion)	$\overline{p} + 3\sqrt{\frac{\overline{p}(1-\overline{p})}{n}}$ or 1.0	$\overline{p} - 3\sqrt{\frac{\overline{p}(1-\overline{p})}{n}}$ or Ø
p' (Percentage)	$\overline{p}' + 3\sqrt{\frac{\overline{p}'(100-\overline{p}')}{n}}$ or 100.0	$\overline{p}' - 3\sqrt{\frac{\overline{p}'(100-\overline{p}')}{n}}$ or Ø
np	$n\overline{p} + 3\sqrt{n\overline{p}(1-\overline{p})}$ or n	$n\overline{p} - 3\sqrt{n\overline{p}(1-\overline{p})}$ or Ø
c	$\overline{c} + 3\sqrt{\overline{c}}$	$\overline{c} - 3\sqrt{\overline{c}}$ or Ø
u	$\overline{u} + 3\sqrt{\frac{\overline{u}}{n}}$	$\overline{u} - 3\sqrt{\frac{\overline{u}}{n}}$ or Ø
X	$\overline{X} + 3\sigma$	$\overline{X} - 3\sigma$
Median, $\tilde{X}$	$\overline{\tilde{X}} + \tilde{A}_2\overline{R}$	$\overline{\tilde{X}} - \tilde{A}_2\overline{R}$

TABLE X.
Minimum Total Runs Above and Below the Median

POINTS ABOVE/ BELOW MEDIAN	MINIMUM RUNS
10	4
11	5
12	6
13	7
14	7
15	8
16	9
17	10
18	10
19	11
20	12
21	13
22	14
23	14
24	15
25	16
26	17
27	18
28	18
29	19
30	20
SOURCE: Same as Run Chart on Table I.	

INDEX

QUALITY AMERICA, INC.®

CONTROL CHARTS FOR AVERAGES AND RANGES

PART NAME		DIMENSION CHARTED					ZERO VALUE	CLASS INTERVAL
PART NUMBER	START DATE	END DATE	UCL AVERAGES	$\bar{\bar{X}}$	LCL AVERAGES	R BAR		UCL RANGES

SAMPLE MEASUREMENTS																										
	1																									
	2																									
	3																									
	4																									
	5																									
SUM																										
AVERAGE, $\bar{X}$																										
RANGE, R																										
		1	2	3	4	5	6	7	8	9	10	11	12	13	14	15	16	17	18	19	20	21	22	23	24	25

AVERAGES

RANGES

QUALITY AMERICA, INC.®

CONTROL CHARTS FOR AVERAGES AND RANGES

PART NAME		DIMENSION CHARTED					ZERO VALUE	CLASS INTERVAL
PART NUMBER	START DATE	END DATE	UCL AVERAGES	$\bar{\bar{X}}$	LCL AVERAGES	R BAR		UCL RANGES

SAMPLE MEASUREMENTS																										
	1																									
	2																									
	3																									
	4																									
	5																									
SUM																										
AVERAGE, $\bar{X}$																										
RANGE, R																										
		1	2	3	4	5	6	7	8	9	10	11	12	13	14	15	16	17	18	19	20	2-	22	23	24	25

AVERAGES

RANGES

QUALITY AMERICA, INC.®

CONTROL CHARTS FOR AVERAGES AND RANGES

PART NAME			DIMENSION CHARTED					ZERO VALUE	CLASS INTERVAL
PART NUMBER	START DATE	END DATE	UCL AVERAGES	$\bar{\bar{X}}$	LCL AVERAGES	R BAR			UCL RANGES

SAMPLE MEASUREMENTS		1	2	3	4	5	6	7	8	9	10	11	12	13	14	15	16	17	18	19	20	21	22	23	24	25
	1																									
	2																									
	3																									
	4																									
	5																									
SUM																										
AVERAGE, $\bar{X}$																										
RANGE, R																										

AVERAGES

RANGES

QUALITY AMERICA, INC.®

CONTROL CHARTS FOR AVERAGES AND RANGES

PART NAME		DIMENSION CHARTED					ZERO VALUE	CLASS INTERVAL
PART NUMBER	START DATE	END DATE	UCL AVERAGES	$\bar{\bar{X}}$	LCL AVERAGES	R BAR		UCL RANGES

SAMPLE MEASUREMENTS		1	2	3	4	5	6	7	8	9	10	11	12	13	14	15	16	17	18	19	20	21	22	23	24	25
	1																									
	2																									
	3																									
	4																									
	5																									
SUM																										
AVERAGE, $\bar{X}$																										
RANGE, R																										

AVERAGES

RANGES

QUALITY AMERICA, INC.®

CONTROL CHARTS FOR AVERAGES AND RANGES

PART NAME			DIMENSION CHARTED				ZERO VALUE	CLASS INTERVAL
PART NUMBER	START DATE	END DATE	UCL AVERAGES	$\bar{\bar{X}}$	LCL AVERAGES	R BAR		UCL RANGES

SAMPLE MEASUREMENTS																									
1																									
2																									
3																									
4																									
5																									
SUM																									
AVERAGE, $\bar{X}$																									
RANGE, R																									
	1	2	3	4	5	6	7	8	9	10	11	12	13	14	15	16	17	18	19	20	21	22	23	24	25

AVERAGES

RANGES

QUALITY AMERICA, INC.®

CONTROL CHARTS FOR AVERAGES AND RANGES

PART NAME	DIMENSION CHARTED				ZERO VALUE	CLASS INTERVAL
PART NUMBER	START DATE	END DATE	UCL AVERAGES	$\bar{\bar{X}}$	LCL AVERAGES	R BAR	UCL RANGES

SAMPLE MEASUREMENTS																										
	1																									
	2																									
	3																									
	4																									
	5																									
SUM																										
AVERAGE, $\bar{X}$																										
RANGE, R																										
		1	2	3	4	5	6	7	8	9	10	11	12	13	14	15	16	17	18	19	20	21	22	23	24	25

AVERAGES

RANGES

Quality America, Inc.®

CALCULATION WORK SHEET

RANGES CHART

Subgroups Included: ____________________

Sum of Ranges = S =

Number of Subgroups = K =

Subgroup Size = n =

Average Range = $\bar{R} = \frac{S}{K}$ = __________ = [ ]

D_3 factor =

$LCL_R = D_3\bar{R}$ = (   )(   ) = [ ]

D_4 factor =

$UCL_R = D_4\bar{R}$ = (   )(   ) = [ ]

AVERAGES CHART

Subgroups Included: ____________________

Sum of Averages = S =

Number of Subgroups = K =

Grand Average = $\bar{\bar{X}} = \frac{S}{K}$ = __________ = [ ]

A_2 factor =

$UCL_{\bar{X}} = \bar{\bar{X}} + A_2\bar{R}$ =   + (   )(   ) = [ ]

$LCL_{\bar{X}} = \bar{\bar{X}} - A_2\bar{R}$ =   − (   )(   ) = [ ]

FACTORS FOR CONTROL LIMITS

n	d_2	D_3	D_4	A_2	$\tilde{A}_2$
2	1.128	0	3.267	1.880	1.880
3	1.693	0	2.575	1.023	1.187
4	2.059	0	2.282	0.729	0.796
5	2.326	0	2.115	0.577	0.691
6	2.534	0	2.004	0.483	0.548
7	2.704	.076	1.924	0.419	0.508
8	2.847	.136	1.864	0.373	0.433
9	2.970	.184	1.816	0.337	0.412
10	3.078	.223	1.777	0.308	0.362

QUALITY AMERICA, INC.®

CALCULATION WORK SHEET

RANGES CHART

Subgroups Included: ______________________

Sum of Ranges = S =

Number of Subgroups = K =

Subgroup Size = n =

Average Range = $\overline{R} = \frac{S}{K}$ = ___________ = ☐

D_3 factor =

$LCL_R = D_3\overline{R}$ = (   )(   ) = ☐

D_4 factor =

$UCL_R = D_4\overline{R}$ = (   )(   ) = ☐

AVERAGES CHART

Subgroups Included: ______________________

Sum of Averages = S =

Number of Subgroups = K =

Grand Average = $\overline{\overline{X}} = \frac{S}{K}$ = ___________ = ☐

A_2 factor =

$UCL_{\overline{X}} = \overline{\overline{X}} + A_2\overline{R}$ =   + (   )(   ) = ☐

$LCL_{\overline{X}} = \overline{\overline{X}} - A_2\overline{R}$ =   − (   )(   ) = ☐

FACTORS FOR CONTROL LIMITS

n	d_2	D_3	D_4	A_2	$\tilde{A}_2$
2	1.128	0	3.267	1.880	1.880
3	1.693	0	2.575	1.023	1.187
4	2.059	0	2.282	0.729	0.796
5	2.326	0	2.115	0.577	0.691
6	2.534	0	2.004	0.483	0.548
7	2.704	.076	1.924	0.419	0.508
8	2.847	.136	1.864	0.373	0.433
9	2.970	.184	1.816	0.337	0.412
10	3.078	.223	1.777	0.308	0.362

QUALITY AMERICA, INC.®

CALCULATION WORK SHEET

RANGES CHART

Subgroups Included: ____________________

Sum of Ranges = S =

Number of Subgroups = K =

Subgroup Size = n =

Average Range = $\overline{R} = \frac{S}{K}$ = __________ = [ ]

D_3 factor =

$LCL_R = D_3\overline{R}$ = (   )(   ) = [ ]

D_4 factor =

$UCL_R = D_4\overline{R}$ = (   )(   ) = [ ]

AVERAGES CHART

Subgroups Included: ____________________

Sum of Averages = S =

Number of Subgroups = K =

Grand Average = $\overline{\overline{X}} = \frac{S}{K}$ = __________ = [ ]

A_2 factor =

$UCL_{\overline{X}} = \overline{\overline{X}} + A_2\overline{R}$ =   + (   )(   ) = [ ]

$LCL_{\overline{X}} = \overline{\overline{X}} - A_2\overline{R}$ =   − (   )(   ) = [ ]

FACTORS FOR CONTROL LIMITS

n	d_2	D_3	D_4	A_2	$\tilde{A}_2$
2	1.128	0	3.267	1.880	1.880
3	1.693	0	2.575	1.023	1.187
4	2.059	0	2.282	0.729	0.796
5	2.326	0	2.115	0.577	0.691
6	2.534	0	2.004	0.483	0.548
7	2.704	.076	1.924	0.419	0.508
8	2.847	.136	1.864	0.373	0.433
9	2.970	.184	1.816	0.337	0.412
10	3.078	.223	1.777	0.308	0.362

RUN CHART

ITEM		ZERO VALUE	CLASS INTERVAL
START DATE	END DATE	MEDIAN	

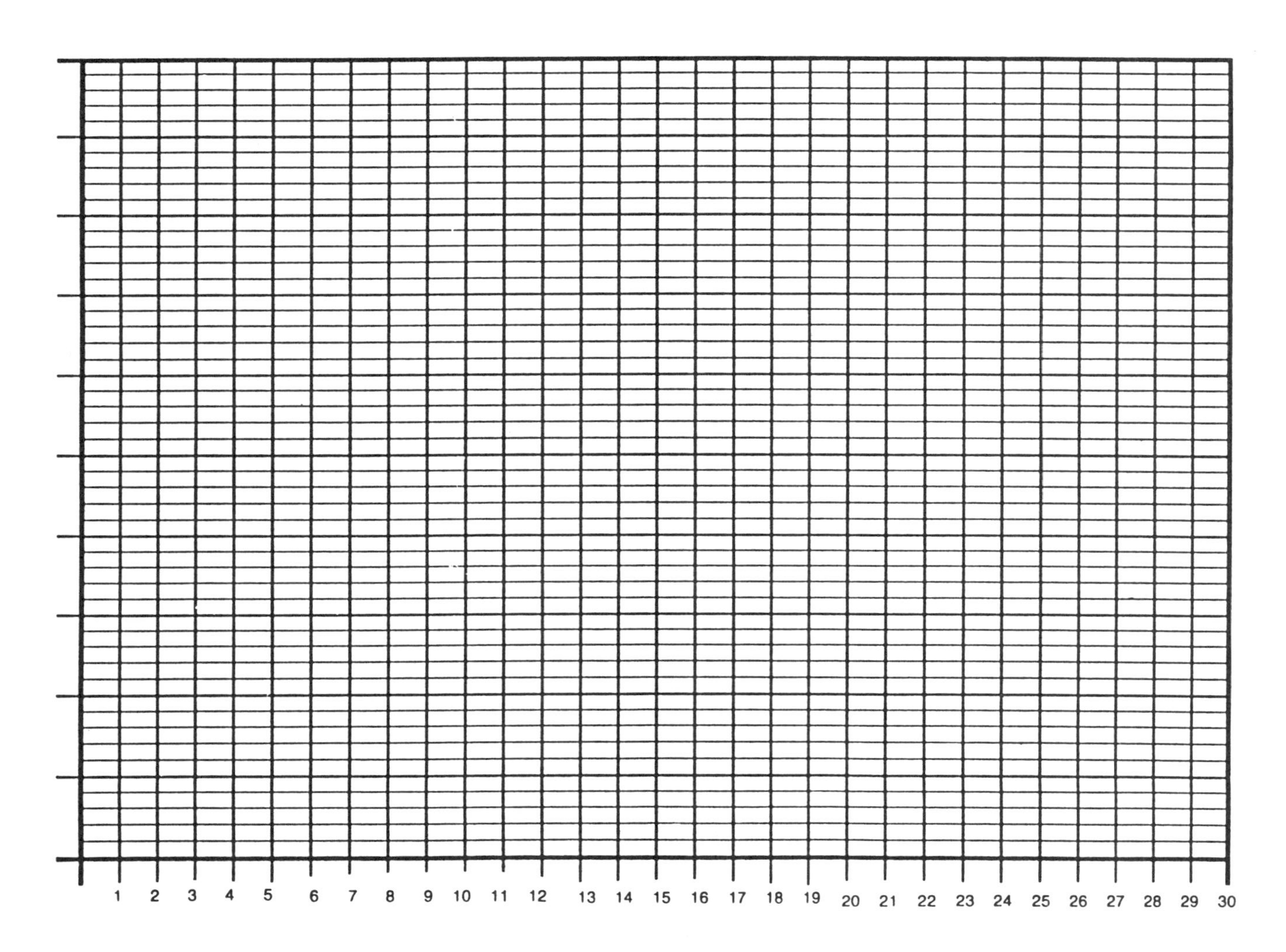

RUN CHART

ITEM		ZERO VALUE	CLASS INTERVAL
START DATE	END DATE	MEDIAN	

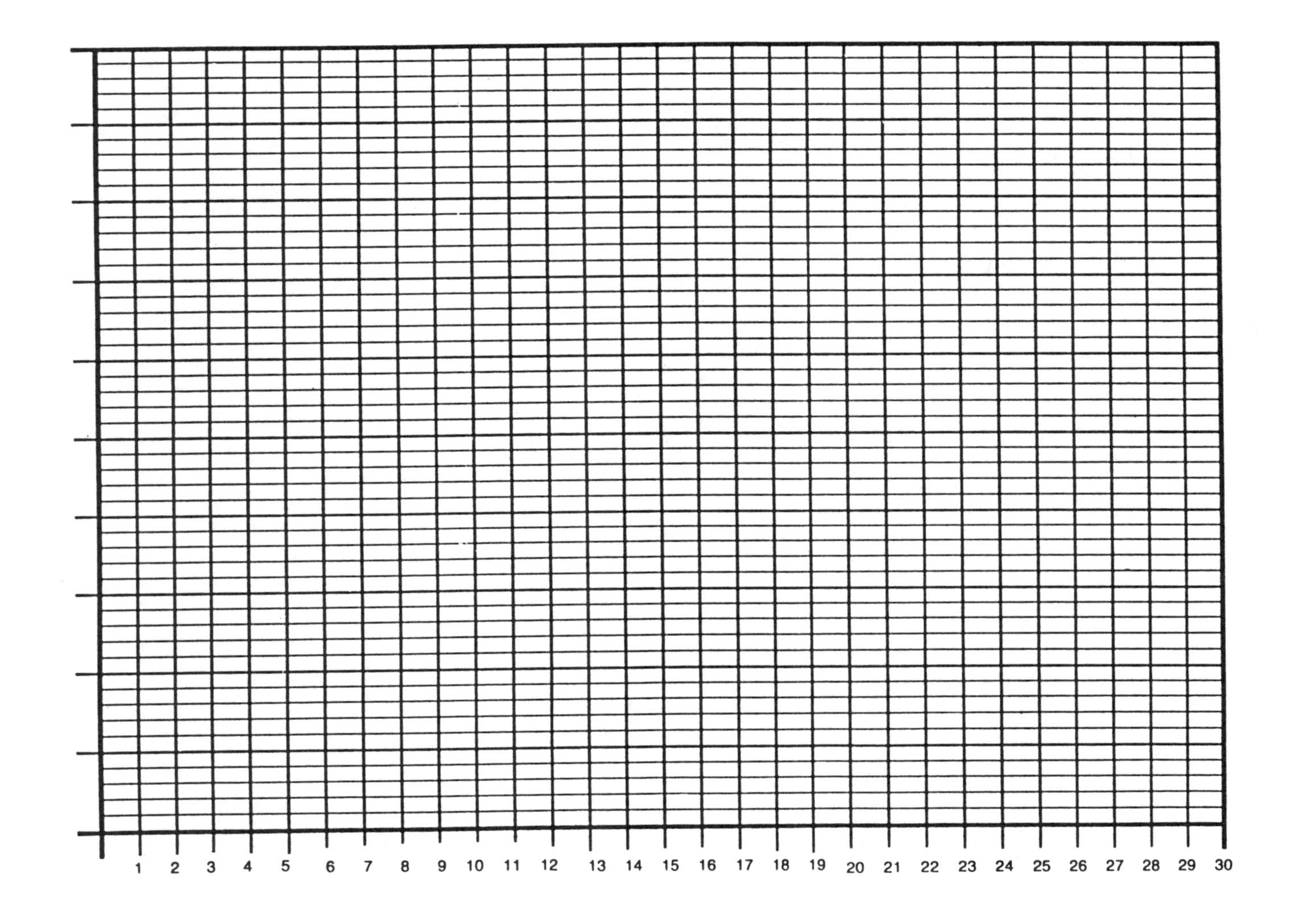

RUN CHART

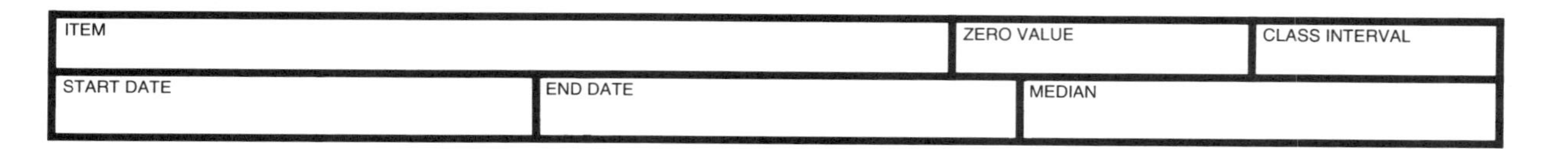

ITEM		ZERO VALUE	CLASS INTERVAL
START DATE	END DATE	MEDIAN	

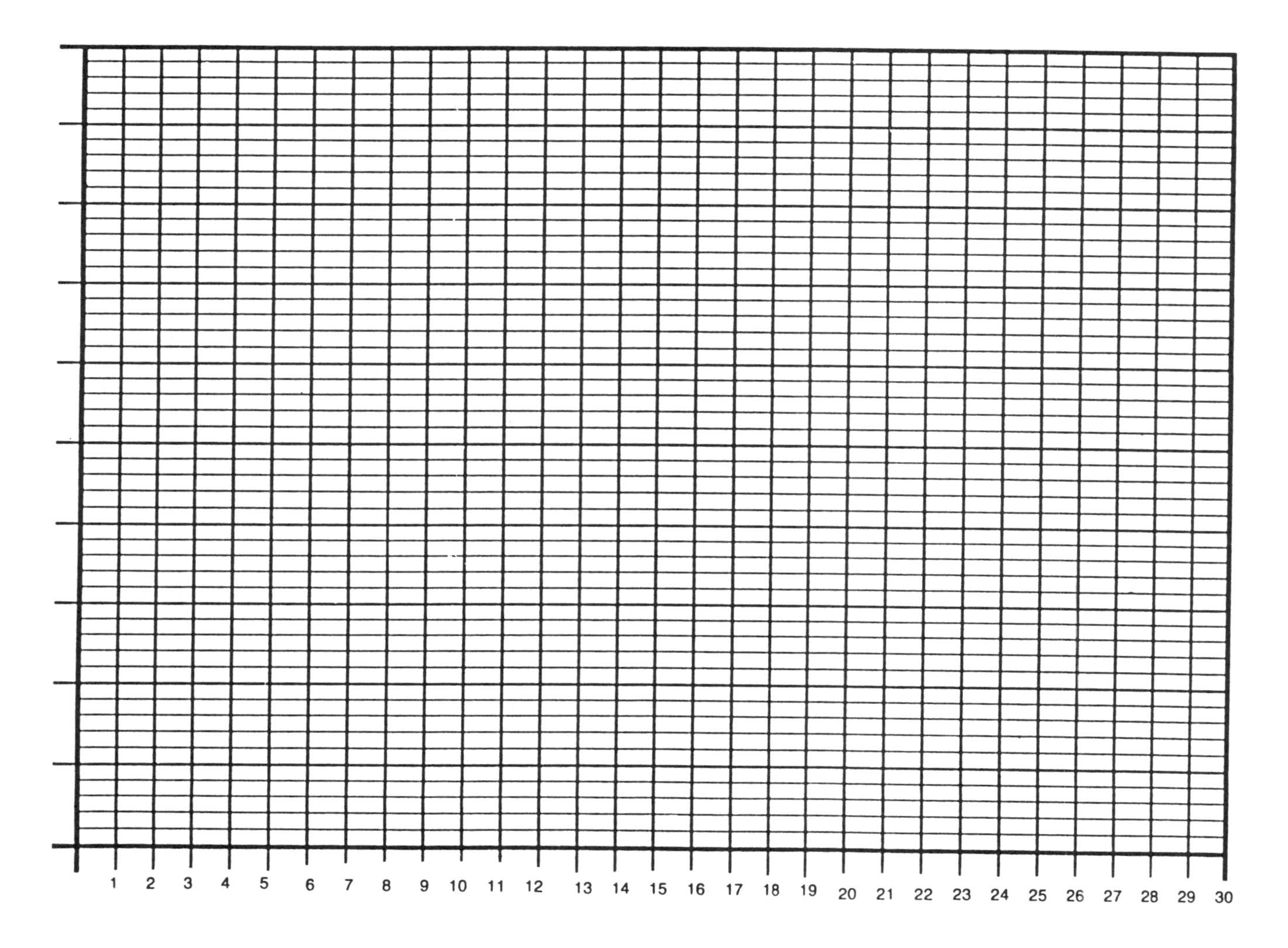

CONTROL CHART FOR MEDIANS

PART NAME		DIMENSION CHARTED			ZERO VALUE	CLASS INTERVAL
PART NUMBER	START DATE	END DATE	UCL MEDIANS	AVERAGE MEDIAN	LCL MEDIANS	MAX. RANGE

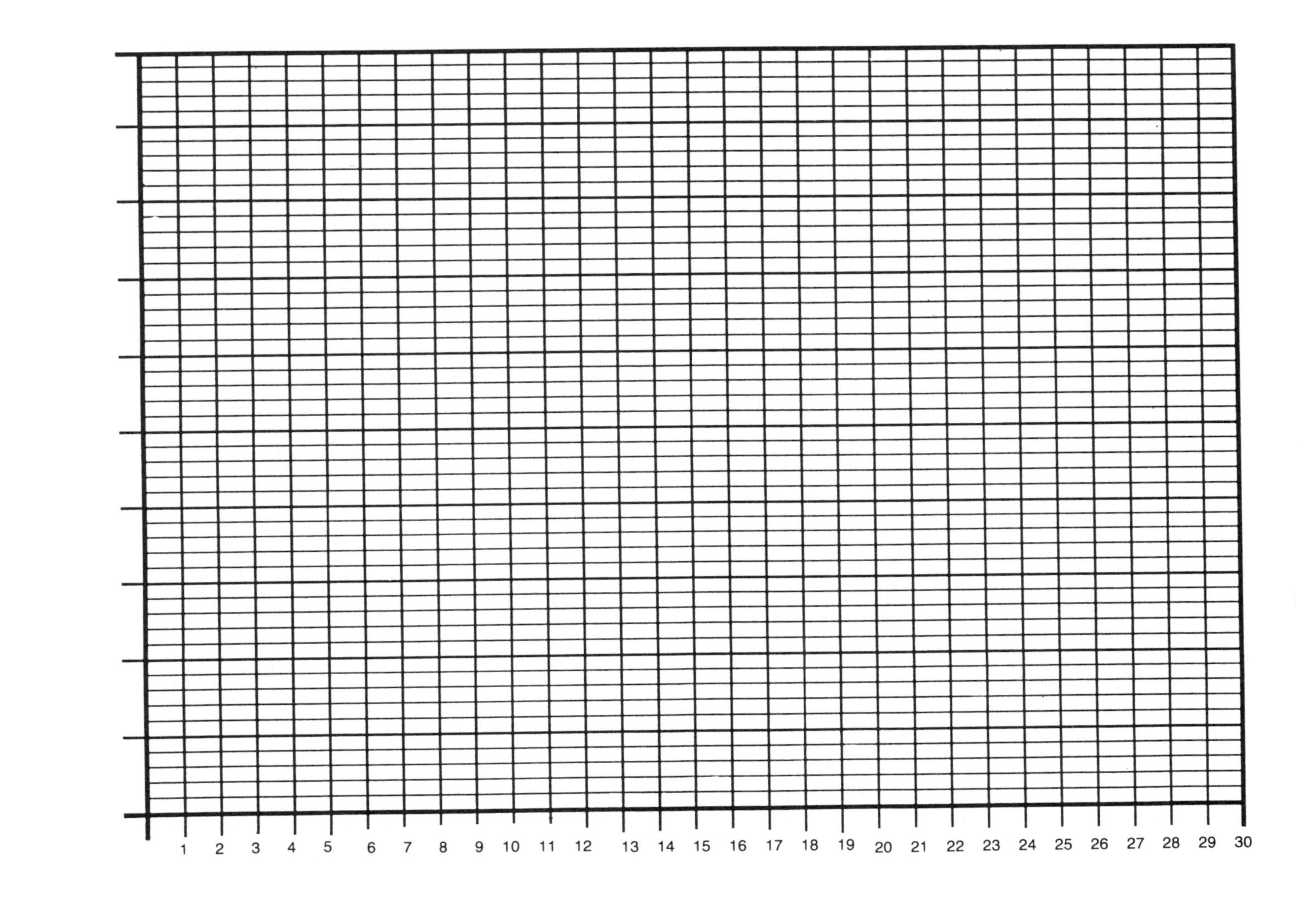

CONTROL CHART FOR MEDIANS

PART NAME			DIMENSION CHARTED			ZERO VALUE	CLASS INTERVAL
PART NUMBER	START DATE		END DATE	UCL MEDIANS	AVERAGE MEDIAN	LCL MEDIANS	MAX. RANGE

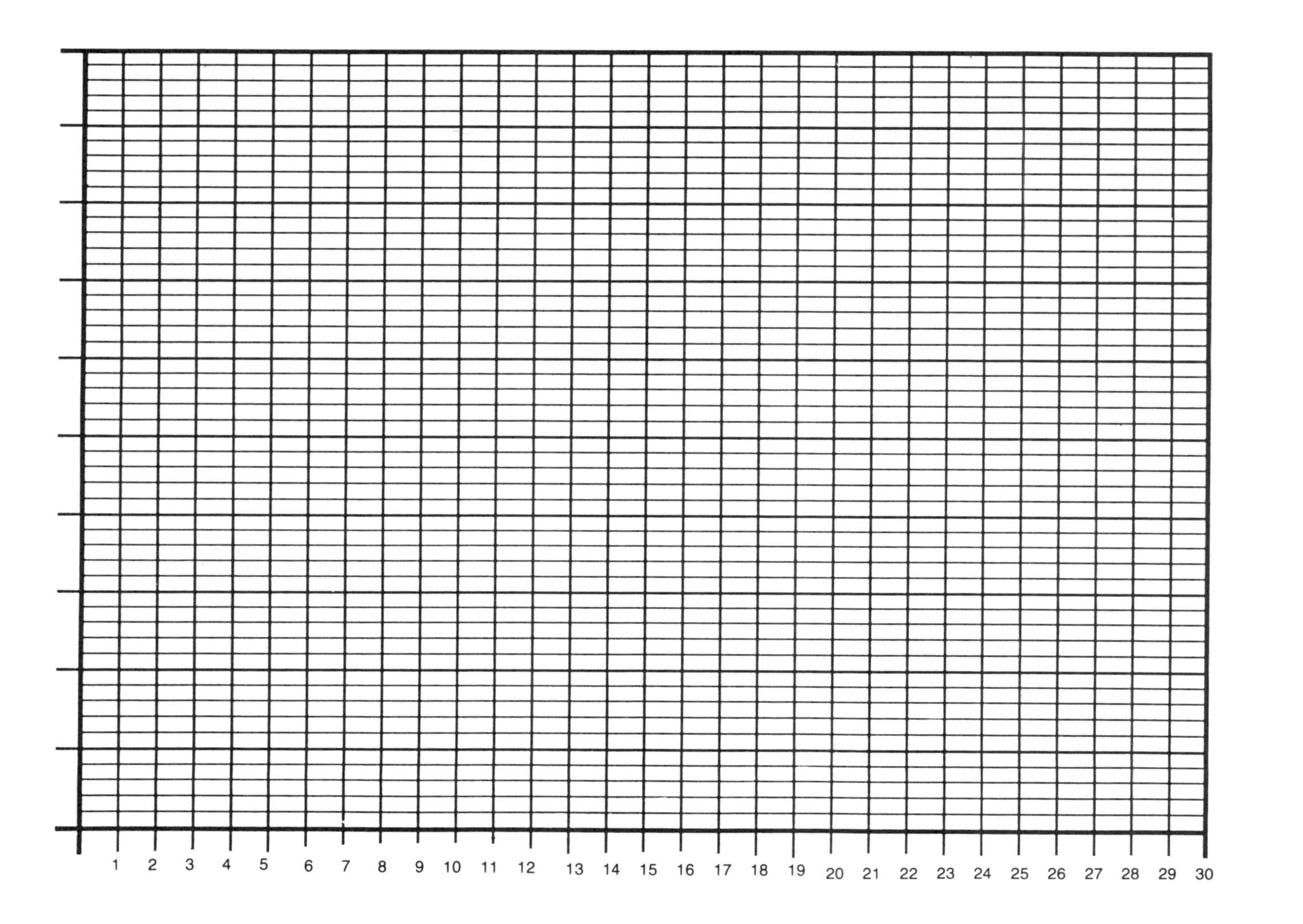

CONTROL CHART FOR MEDIANS

PART NAME		DIMENSION CHARTED			ZERO VALUE	CLASS INTERVAL
PART NUMBER	START DATE	END DATE	UCL MEDIANS	AVERAGE MEDIAN	LCL MEDIANS	MAX. RANGE

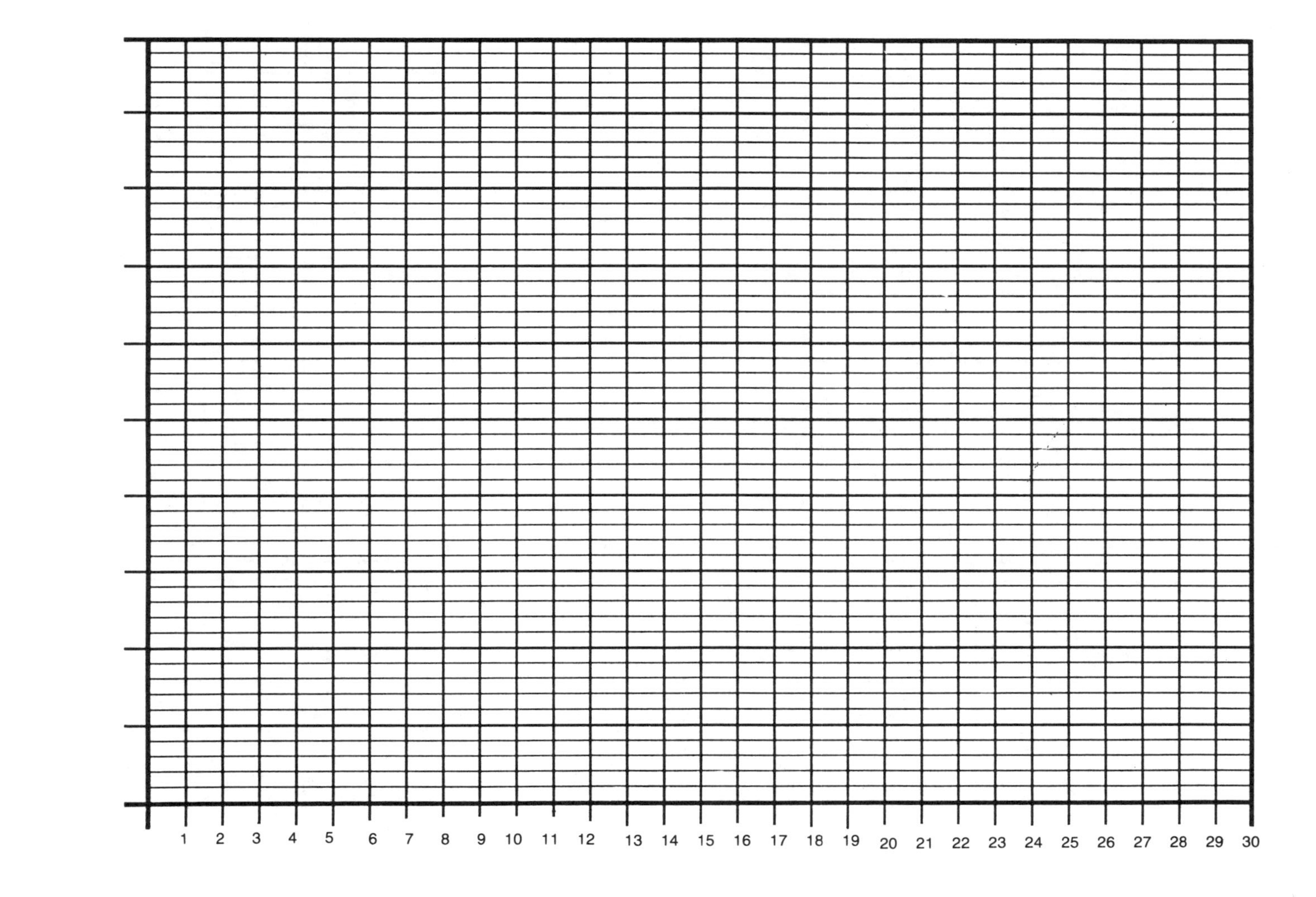

QUALITY AMERICA, INC.®

CONTROL CHART FOR ATTRIBUTE DATA

PLANT	p ☐ np ☐ c ☐ u ☐	PRODUCT ENGINEERING DESIGNATED CONTROL ITEM (∇) YES ☐ NO ☐	PART NUMBER AND NAME
DEPARTMENT	OPERATION NUMBER AND NAME	Avg.— UCL— LCL—	DATE CONTROL LIMITS CALCULATED:

Date

Type of Discrepancy

1.
2.
3.
4.
5.
6.
7.
8.
9.
10.

Total Discrepancies

Average/% Discrepancies

Sample Size (n)

ANY CHANGE IN PEOPLE, EQUIPMENT, MATERIALS, METHODS OR ENVIRONMENT SHOULD BE NOTED ON THE REVERSE SIDE.
THESE NOTES WILL HELP YOU TO TAKE CORRECTIVE OR PROCESS IMPROVEMENT ACTION WHEN SIGNALED BY THE CONTROL CHART.

CONTROL CHART FOR ATTRIBUTE DATA

PLANT	p ☐ c ☐ np ☐ u ☐	PRODUCT ENGINEERING DESIGNATED CONTROL ITEM (∇) YES ☐ NO ☐	PART NUMBER AND NAME
DEPARTMENT	OPERATION NUMBER AND NAME	Avg.— UCL— LCL—	DATE CONTROL LIMITS CALCULATED:

Date																											
Type of Discrepancy																											
1.																											
2.																											
3.																											
4.																											
5.																											
6.																											
7.																											
8.																											
9.																											
10.																											
Total Discrepancies																											
Average/% Discrepancies																											
Sample Size (n)																											

ANY CHANGE IN PEOPLE, EQUIPMENT, MATERIALS, METHODS OR ENVIRONMENT SHOULD BE NOTED ON THE REVERSE SIDE.
THESE NOTES WILL HELP YOU TO TAKE CORRECTIVE OR PROCESS IMPROVEMENT ACTION WHEN SIGNALED BY THE CONTROL CHART.

QUALITY AMERICA, INC.®

CONTROL CHART FOR ATTRIBUTE DATA

PLANT	p ☐ np ☐ c ☐ u ☐	PRODUCT ENGINEERING DESIGNATED CONTROL ITEM (∇) YES ☐ NO ☐	PART NUMBER AND NAME
DEPARTMENT	OPERATION NUMBER AND NAME	Avg.= UCL= LCL=	DATE CONTROL LIMITS CALCULATED:

Date
Type of Discrepancy
1.
2.
3.
4.
5.
6.
7.
8.
9.
10.
Total Discrepancies
Average/% Discrepancies
Sample Size (n)

ANY CHANGE IN PEOPLE, EQUIPMENT, MATERIALS, METHODS OR ENVIRONMENT SHOULD BE NOTED ON THE REVERSE SIDE.
THESE NOTES WILL HELP YOU TO TAKE CORRECTIVE OR PROCESS IMPROVEMENT ACTION WHEN SIGNALED BY THE CONTROL CHART.

CQE Examination Study Guide

If you are preparing for the ASQC Certified Quality Engineer's examination, or if you are simply interested in developing a comprehensive understanding of Quality Engineering, you are faced with a formidable task. Quality Engineering is a vast field that encompasses many other disciplines. Until now the aspiring Quality Engineer had to find his own way through this mass of material, hoping that he allocated his time to the correct subjects.

The proof that this method was, at best, questionable is that nearly 50% of all who take the CQE examination fail. This fact bothered Thomas Pyzdek, who had taught CQE refresher classes for colleges and business clients in Arizona. It bothered him because he saw between 80% and 100% of his students pass the CQE examination on their first attempt. He knew that one reason was that the CQE refresher course helped these people focus their attention to the most important topics. It disturbed him that many qualified CQE candidates were being unfairly deprived of their certification simply because they didn't have access to a qualified instructor.

His answer to this problem was the *CQE Examination Study Guide*. Pyzdek condensed all of his course materials into this book, including

- CQE refresher course outline, syllabus, and reading list.
- Multiple choice quizzes and answers.
- A final exam that simulates the real CQE exam.
- The ASQC certification program booklet.
- All previously published CQE exams.

In addition, the book includes **complete, detailed answers to all 170 questions in the CQE exam published in the July 1984 issue of *Quality Progress* magazine!** Along with the answers the book provides references for further study. The references go beyond just naming books.

It tells you which sections should be mastered. Also included are references to important articles in magazines or technical journals. In short, it's a lot like being in a CQE Refresher Class!

Order your copy of the CQE *Examination Study Guide* today!

#QAB002

#MDB021

Considerations of Quality play a prominent role in all fields — particularly with recently focused attention on issues of consumerism, product and professional liability, and government regulation. American industries must improve quality if they are to remain competitive in world markets.

What Every Engineer Should Know About Quality Control

The engineering community occupies a vital function in the effort to advance quality — namely, that designs be well engineered for consistent reproduction. Wading through the vast body of available information to form a compact, up-to-date treatment of the essentials of quality control, ***What Every Engineer Should Know About Quality Control***

- **surveys significant features of quality control from the perspective of a practicing quality professional** — providing engineers with the fundamental elements of quality and how they work in actual practice
- **shows how to implement quality programs from beginning to end** — supplying practical, perceptive information for companies that seek to create their own quality programs
- **introduces statistical methods used in quality control and gives examples of how they are applied to quality control situations** — combining both theory and applications for a well-rounded, succinct look at the topic
- **discusses both technical and non technical aspects of quality control** — showing how quality control encompasses such diverse disciplines as mathematics, management, psychology, engineering, law, and human relations, all of which are necessary for success.

Useful to both professionals and students, ***What Every Engineer Should Know About Quality Control*** contains drawings, equations, and tables, and is ideal reading for all engineers concerned with quality and product assurance, manufacturing and production managers, and upper-level undergraduate courses in industrial, civil, mechanical, electrical and ceramic engineering.

As a quality expert Tom Pyzdek, Quality America's founder and president, has known for years that normal distributions were anything but normal. *That's why we included the ability to handle non-normal data in QA's very first software package in 1983*. Our users loved it. Recently, our competitors have joined us in recognizing the importance of this feature. It seems that non-normal data analysis is suddenly everyone's "new feature."

Over the years we have continued to improve our ability to handle non-normal data. SPC-PC II includes The *Data Tailor*™ which automatically finds the curve that best fits your data. SPC-PC II then uses the curve to analyze long-term yields and to compute all capability indices correctly. The Data Tailor is very easy to use; in fact, you don't have to do a thing!

The Data Tailor also has the ability to correctly analyze ANSI Y14.5 data such as concentricity, flatness, straightness, and many other "folded data" characteristics. Such data are very familiar to anyone involved in mechanical inspection or the aerospace business. The Data Tailor will never embarass you by showing negative numbers on charts when they can't possibly exist.

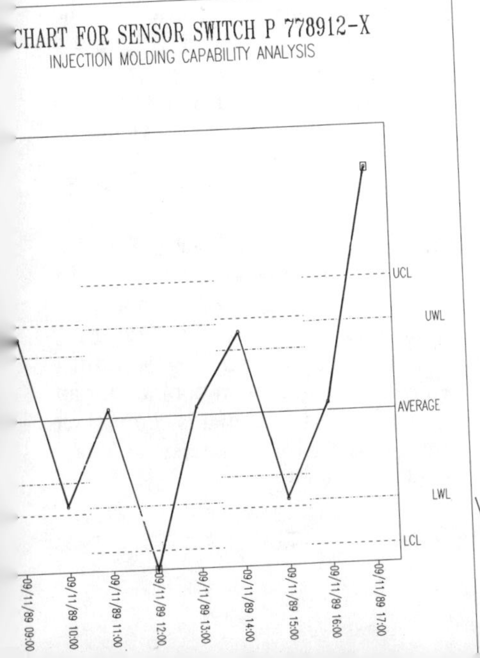

Of course, data is useless if you don't know where it came from, so we created *QDM*™, a powerful SPC data management system. With QDM a single file can contain information on up to five variables or attributes. In addition to complete titles and subtitles for each variable, you can also store up to 16 user-defined fields describing each variable. Also stored with the data are all of your options, so you don't have to remember the settings you used to produce last month's charts.

Our prices are so low that many people ask if anything is left out: nothing is. Why wait? Call **1-800-729-0867** and place your order today!

Hardware Requirements

SPC-PC II runs on MS-DOS systems with a minimum of 640k RAM. The DOS version must be 3.0 or higher. Requires hard disk.

30 day money back guarantee.

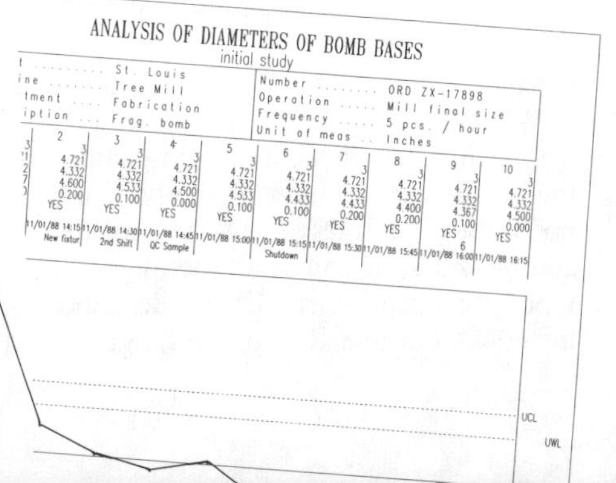

SUMMARY

ROUTINES

X Bar, R Charts
X Bar, Sigma Charts
X charts (individual)
Moving Average, Range
Moving Average, Sigma
Histograms/ Capability Analysis
CuSum Charts
Multi-variate Control Charts
p, np Charts for Several Attributes
c, u Charts for Several Attributes
Scatter plots/Regression Analysis
Pareto Analysis

ANALYSIS OPTIONS

User Defined Limits
Analyze Part of a File
Keep/Drop Out-of-Control Data
Subgroups of 99 on X Bar charts
Missing data on X Bar charts
Normal or Non-Normal Data
C_{pk}, C_p, C_R, Z_L, Z_U, C_{pm}
% Above and % Below Specs.
Process Performance Indices
Automatically Analyzes Last Set Number of Groups

OTHER FEATURES

Pull-down Menus
Context-sensitive HELP
Presentation Quality Graphics
Macros
Export Charts to WordPerfect 5.0
Export Charts to Ventura Pub.
User Selectable Fonts
Batch Printing of Graphics
No Fixed Limit on File Sizes
Up to 5 Variables in a Single File
Import Data from Spreadsheets
Import Data from databases
Network Support
Written in C

PYZDEK'S Guide to SPC

About the Book

PYZDEK'S GUIDE TO SPC is written by Quality America's Founder and President, Thomas Pyzdek. It is co-published by Quality America and ASQC Quality Press. The book is part of a series based on materials used in ASQC seminars on SPC. Volume Onc, *Fundamentals*, provides information that everyone using SPC should know. Topics include organizing and implementing SPC; group dynamics; data collection; problem solving techniques (including cause & effect diagrams and flowcharts); Pareto analysis; histograms; scatter plots; run charts; x bar, R, and sigma charts; p, np, c, and u charts. The subject matter is presented in a text with an accompanying workbook to allow the reader to practice his or her new knowledge. Instructor's materials are also available. Included are 120 professionally prepared 2 color mylar overhead visuals in an attractive case. Also included is an Instructor's booklet with annotations for each overhead visual and a discussion of workbook exercises. These allow the instructor and the student the opportunity to fully explore each topic. Later volumes in the series will include Volume Two, *Applications and Special Techniques* and Volume Three, *Advanced Topics.*

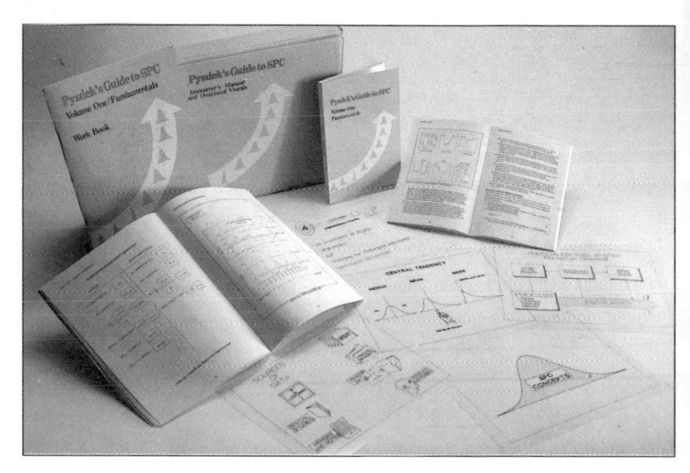

About the Author

Experience

For over 22 years Thomas Pyzdek has used SPC to improve quality and productivity for his employers and consulting clients, as well as in his own business operations. He's had hands-on experience with applications ranging from machine shops to chemical processes to service. This experience is evident on nearly every page of *Pyzdek's Guide to SPC.*

Teaching

Pyzdek taught his first class more than 15 years ago. Since then he has conducted hundreds of SPC seminars, both public seminars and on-site seminars, for thousands of students. Pyzdek has taught ASQC's course in SP/QC nationally for several years.

Writing

The author of the best-selling *An SPC Primer*, Pyzdek's writing style is famous for making difficult information easy to understand. Other books by Pyzdek include *The CQE Examination Study Guide* and *What Every Engineer Should Know About Quality Control.*

#QAB005 (Text)
#QAB006 (Workbook)
#QAB007 (Inst. Materials)

An SPC Primer *SPC Self-Teaching Guide*

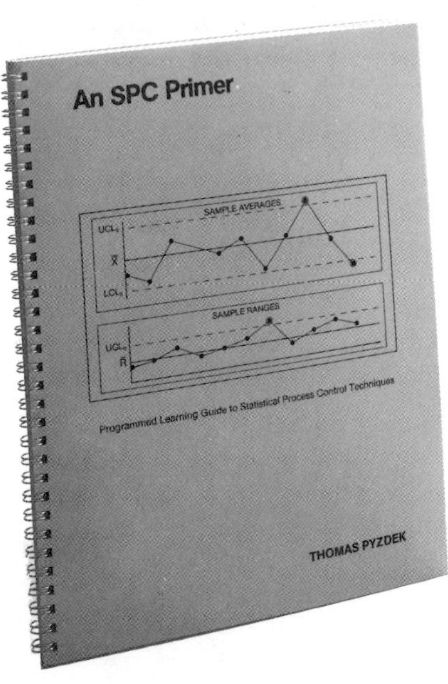

#QAB001

We learned that SPC need not be difficult to understand. In fact, we discovered, if the material is properly presented, SPC is so easy to understand it's simply amazing! The *SPC Primer* is a self-study book based on years of experience with the application and teaching of SPC. It is written in programmed learning format and it is designed to allow the reader to learn SPC at his or her own pace. Students begin with basic arithmetic and move ahead in small steps with constant feedback in the form of exercises. We've learned that SPC is not a spectator sport, and the *SPC Primer* makes sure that the student ***knows*** the material before allowing him to move ahead.

While the *SPC Primer* begins at a very elementary level, it doesn't insult the intelligence of the reader. There are no cartoons or cutesy drawings, just a complete description of all the major types of control charts. Charts described include X bar and R, moving range control charts for individuals, run charts, p charts, np charts, c charts and u charts. The book not only describes the construction of the charts, but their application as well. Also described are such important related topics as run tests, tests of normality, the central limit theorem and its importance in SPC, and process capability analysis. The Cp index is described in detail. An appendix with blank forms and worksheets is included.

Perhaps the most important evidence of the value of this book is the fact that it has been used by thousands of companies to train their employees. The book is in use by nearly every major firm in the United States, as well as many foreign countries. The *SPC Primer* is now in its eleventh printing, and still going strong. If you are looking for an introduction to SPC that is comprehensive but still easy to understand, this book is for you!